John Fenton

Early Hebrew Life

A Study in Sociology

John Fenton

Early Hebrew Life
A Study in Sociology

ISBN/EAN: 9783337414634

Printed in Europe, USA, Canada, Australia, Japan

Cover: Foto ©Suzi / pixelio.de

More available books at **www.hansebooks.com**

EARLY HEBREW LIFE:

A STUDY IN SOCIOLOGY.

BY

JOHN FENTON.

LONDON:

TRUBNER & CO., LUDGATE HILL.

1880.

TO

HEINRICH EWALD.

———

𝕿𝖍𝖊 𝕷𝖊𝖆𝖗𝖓𝖊𝖗 𝖙𝖔 𝖙𝖍𝖊 𝕸𝖆𝖘𝖙𝖊𝖗.

PREFACE.

THE title of this little book is, I think, a sufficient indication of its contents: all that is here necessary is a brief explanation of the relation in which my results stand towards those of the school of historic or literary criticism.

Books which, like the Pentateuch, treat of the laws and customs of a people, have a double aspect. In their literary aspect they require to be investigated with regard to form rather than to matter. Not that the matter is of no importance, but it is of an importance subordinate to that of the form; for the critic endeavours to ascertain the currents of popular thought, and feeling, and aim which produced the book he is criticising, and these he learns oftenest from incidental expressions or from curious turns and applications made of old laws and customs. Hence he desires not to strip a custom of its adventitious surroundings, but rather to examine

b

these as the material whence the desired result is obtained.

Viewed again in a sociological aspect, such books as the Pentateuch require to be studied almost entirely with regard to their matter. The question from this point of view is one, not of ascertaining the popular mind at that particular crisis of history when the Pentateuch (or rather, some one of its component parts) chanced to be written, but of ascertaining the period of social progress at which any one custom first came into life. This can be ascertained only by comparing the custom with the analogous customs of other peoples, and so fitting it into the niche it occupies in the order of social development. But to do this it is necessary to consider, not the accidental form, but the essential germ of the custom; and thus much of the form becomes unessential to the sociologist.

This may be illustrated by the twofold aspect of the sabbatic year of the Hebrews. Of this institution Dr. Kuenen says that it "displays the priestly notions on the ownership of land." "The priestly lawgiver's chief object was the maintenance of the hereditary ownership of land. With this in view, he thinks he must confine within very narrow limits the right of an individual to dispose freely of his property. Or rather, he does not allow the indi-

vidual any property in the strict sense of the word."
And he speaks also of "the high estimation of rest,
as such, which pervades the priestly·Sabbath-com-
mandments."[1]

This is a purely literary interpretation of the
passages, and no doubt it is a fair inference from
the expressions "Sabbath of rest," "year of rest,"
"the land did not keep her Sabbaths," and the like.
And this interpretation is based upon the incidental
expressions which indicate the mental bias of the
writer of Leviticus. Had that author simply said,
"The land shall lie fallow every seven years," it
would have been difficult to ascertain the exact
feelings with which he regarded it. And as a
factor towards determining the circumstances under
which Leviticus was written, the law, so expressed,
would have been of little value.

Sociologically, however, as is shown in § 31 of this
essay, the simple law of the periodical fallow is the
essential point of the enactment. Whether the
period was one year or seven, whether the legislator
regarded it as a religious institution or not, whether
he called it a "Sabbath rest" or a "fallow," are
matters of comparatively small consequence. They
will affect our judgment as to the original or derived
form of the law, but they do not affect the funda-

[1] Kuenen, *Religion of Israel*, E.T., ii. 281, 283.

mental point of the *periodicity of the fallow,* which
at once determines the sociological category and age
of the law.

That these two aspects are distinct from each
other is not sufficiently observed. It by no means
follows as a matter of course that the rise of a custom
or law is contemporaneous with its appearance in
history. Many forces may conspire to retard its
appearance in legal works. Suppose, for instance,
a book to be written with the intention of simply
settling certain disputed questions. The writer may
choose not to complicate his subject by introducing
undisputed customs. After him there may come
another with the opposite desire of writing a com-
pendium; and naturally he inserts the custom which
his predecessor had omitted; and so the custom
earlier in point of usage becomes later in point of
record. Or again, a code of laws is struggling into
authority, and suffers mutilation and alteration according to the usages of the various tribes or castes
among whom it is introduced. And so some one
part of it becomes simultaneously altered in various
ways; and when centuries have passed, strangers
finding variant copies of the code, meet the strange
spectacle of a younger edition containing a more
archaic custom than an older one. Such an instance
is before me now. The Hindu code known by the

name of Manu is substantially the same as several
other codes, one of which bears the name of Yajnavalkya. Now Manu is in all probability pre-Buddhistic
in date; Yajnavalkya is undoubtedly post-Buddhistic.
And Dr. Stenzler, the learned editor of Yajnavalkya,
gives very cogent reasons for believing that work to
be a later recension than Manu. Yet what do we
find? That while in many points Manu preserves
the more archaic forms of such customs as the levirate,
the procreation of sons from a widow and the like,
Yajnavalkya has preserved the more archaic form of
the law of inheritance; inheritance by children jointly
being, I need hardly say, a much older custom than
primogeniture:—

Manu.	*Yajnavalkya.*
ix. 104, 105. "After the death of the father and mother, the brothers being assembled, may divide among themselves the paternal estate. . . . The eldest brother may take entire possession of the estate, and the others may live under him."	ii. 117. "After the death of both parents the sons shall *divide equally* the property and debts."
112–117. Either a preliminary deduction is to be made for the first-born, or else "let the eldest have a double share."	ii. 114. "When a father divides the inheritance, he may divide it according to his own pleasure; either he may give the eldest son the better portion, *or all may receive equal shares.*"

This is conclusive evidence of the independence
of the two lines of research. It is not possible to
infer immediately from the literary date of a custom

its sociological date; nor is it possible to infer from the known date of the institution of a custom that the record of it is of the same date. The two are distinct, and inferences drawn from one with regard to the other will certainly be contradictory. Hence it is that, while Dr. Kuenen's literary conclusions as to the feelings of the legislator of the sabbatic year are unobjectionable, his sociological inference that "his ordinance sounds very well in theory, but practically it is impossible," [1] is altogether inadmissible. In drawing that inference he does but follow Bertheau, who says: "If I am to describe the impression made upon me by this collection [*i.e.*, the legislation in Exodus, Numbers, and Leviticus], I must say that many of its laws are intended for a state in process of formation. Institutions like the Sabbath and jubilee years, Levitical cities and cities of refuge, are more easily set up in such than in a state where old tenures and vested interests require to be respected and reserved." [2] If I am to describe the impression made upon me by this idea of the contemporaneous existence of the Sabbath and jubilee years in *a state in process of formation*, I must say that the darkness of pre-anthropologic times was Egyptian indeed.

[1] Kuenen, *Religion of Israel*, ii. 283.
[2] Bertheau, *Die Sieben Gruppen Mosaischer Gesetze*, 288.

That Bertheau, writing forty years ago, should have erred, is not surprising, but one is certainly astonished at the *à priori* explanations given of ordinary laws like that of the fruit trees in Deut. xx. 19 (see § 24). "As if to show," says Dr. Kuenen, " that this commandment [that of cutting off the other nations in ver. 17] is not prompted by bloodthirstiness or cruelty, the author immediately adds that if a foreign city is besieged a long time, the fruit trees are not to be cut down!"[1] And similarly Dr. Colenso adduces this, after several others,'as "another instance of the tender-heartedness of the Deuteronomist."[2] If such explanations must be offered, it would surely be equally apt if we regarded the law as the outcome of the carnal self-seeking, or personal equation of some rural priest, who, like the herdsman-prophet of Tekoa, found his chief enjoyment in " planting vineyards and drinking the wine thereof, and making gardens and eating the fruit of them."

The fundamental error of all such explanations is the confusion between social and individual feelings. Tender-heartedness, care for the poor, desire for the maintenance of families, are no monopoly of the Hebrew code. The same characteristics occur in

---

[1] *Religion of Israel*, ii. 24.
[2] *Crit. Exam. of the Pentateuch*, pt. vi. 408, 445.

every code, but they occur not by reason of the individual eccentricities of the lawgivers, but from the necessities of social life. When one is dependent for one's green food upon the produce of the communal orchard, it is simply bad policy to allow oneself to be hurried by the desire for the speedy capture of a town into doing an act which will recoil on one's own head when one occupies the town. So with the poor. When a bad season or a poor allotment in the common field may throw a villager upon the mercy of his fellows, the result is naturally a species of simple poor-law, which latter, by the way, in its developed form, is considered by many to be the product of anything but tenderheartedness.

But these errors are nothing compared with the diametrical contradiction between Dr. Goldziher and Dr. Wellhausen. It is well known that the former scholar, who is usually held to have satisfactorily solarised the patriarchs, bases his argument upon the fact that nomadism or pastoral life influenced Hebrew life and mythology at an earlier period than agriculture, which they did not attain to until later.[1] But hear Dr. Wellhausen upon the relative position of tithes of cattle, which are pastoral chattels, and tithes of corn, and wine, and oil, which are agricul-

[1] Goldziher, *Der Mythos bei den Hebräern*, chap. iv.

tural chattels: " Altogether unprecedented (wahrhaft unerhört) is it that in the priestly codex the
tithe, which, in the nature of things, can only attach
to substances of solid measure, like corn, wine, and
oil, is extended to cattle, so that, in addition to the
human first-born, the tithe of oxen and sheep must
also be paid to the priests."[1]

From which it appears that while in matters of
mythology the Hebrews progressed from nomadism
to agriculture, in religion they progressed from agriculture to nomadism. How far I agree with Dr.
Goldziher's division of the periods of progress the
pages which follow will show. Of Dr. Wellhausen's
extraordinary doctrine that tithes of cattle are never
found, and his still more extraordinary reason,
because cattle cannot be counted, one can only say
that without doubt it is " wahrhaft unerhört."
Either the doctrine or the reason, if one or the other
can be proved from the Pentateuch, may be com-
mended to divines of the older school as amply sufficient to relegate Hebrew history to the domain of
the miraculous, and very probably to remove it from
the category of humanity altogether.

After all, it is not wonderful that, living as we do
in an age of somewhat advanced culture, we should
sometimes fail to refer to true social causes, laws

[1] Wellhausen, *Geschichte Israels*, i. 162.

which, if proposed to-day, would certainly be thought to be the product of individual peculiarities. And therefore my free criticism of the leaders of the newer school of Hebrew learning will not, I trust, be attributed to a desire to depreciate their labours. It would, indeed, ill become me to speak disrespectfully of men to whom I owe much, and to whose learning my own is nowise comparable. But in this one point I believe them to be in error, and in an error which, if not clearly indicated, may lead to disastrous results. And an additional advantage in grouping all my polemic here is that the reader knows at the outset how far I differ from current criticism, and I am consequently relieved from the necessity of interrupting the even tenor of the exposition by refutory discussions.

With respect to the exposition itself, I have sometimes been doubtful whether in seeking to be brief I may not have become obscure. The plan of the book obliged me to confine statements of principle in as short a space as possible. To have elaborated them fully would have been to write, not a *Study of Early Hebrew Life*, but a *Principles of Sociology with especial reference to the Hebrews*, a work which I by no means desire to undertake. Moreover, as the principles on which I rely are those generally accepted, a long elaboration of them was unnecessary. It seemed better to refer the reader to the works of known leaders rather than to supersede those works by inferior re-statements of my own. Only in a few instances, where it was necessary to re-state or re-illustrate a principle, have I entered into detail. Otherwise I have stated my principles with the utmost brevity; and if the reader is inclined to question any of them, he will find in the margin sufficient authority quoted for reference. At the same time, I have myself verified, and am quite prepared to defend, all my positions.

With these explanations I will leave the work to speak for itself.

J. F.

CONTENTS.

—————

I.—INTRODUCTORY.

II.—THE NOMAD PERIOD.

III.—THE PASTORAL PERIOD.

IV.—THE SETTLED OR AGRICULTURAL PERIOD.

ADDENDUM.

Additional Note on the " Migrash," p. 37.

In treating of the *Migrash* I admitted, with reference to its avail-
ability for cattle, that it might be used "partly for pasture." It
escaped me at the time that, in some tribes who are still in the
transition stage from pastoral to agricultural life, the smaller and
younger cattle are kept in enclosures near to the huts, while the larger
cattle pasture on the waste. The Hassanyeh Arabs of the Soudan
are an instance. Still migratory, with large herds of cattle, they
cultivate grain, millet, and corn during the rainy season. Their
cattle, sheep, and goats browse in the open plain. The villages consist of two long rows of huts with a street between them, and *behind
each hut is a small enclosure of dry thorns serving as a pen or fold for
the calves and lambs.* The enclosure for the great cattle is the joint
work of the tribesmen (Petherick, *Egypt, the Soudan, &c.*, 135, 148,
169). No doubt the Hebrew *Migrash* was used for similar purposes.

EARLY HEBREW LIFE.

I.—Introductory.

§ 1. THE traditions of the Old Testament present to us the Hebrews as having passed through two stages of social development, the pastoral and the agricultural. The legends of the patriarchs picture them as shepherds dwelling in tents, and moving from region to region as one spot or another offers better pasture for their flocks and herds. But as the traditions pass along the course of time the colouring visibly changes—the tent merges into the hut, and the hut expands into cities and palaces; cornfields, vineyards, and oliveyards are the scene of the traditions; the flocks and herds fall gradually into the background, till they become the distinctive attribute of two individual tribes, and finally are altogether lost sight of in the extensive commerce of the days of Solomon.

The verisimilitude of the picture is undeniable. The literal truth of the patriarchal legends is doubted by many, but none doubt the truth of the social growth which the Pentateuch depicts.

Like progress is found in other societies.

§ 2. In this gradual progress the evolution of the Hebrews has but followed the same lines as the evolution of the other families of mankind. Within the circle of the Aryan languages the same progress from pastoral to agricultural life is traceable. Not only is there the negative evidence from the non-possession by the race of a common vocabulary for agricultural occupations, but the positive evidence

Aryan societies.

from institutions. In India the Rig-Veda exalts cattle as the great means of subsistence, and is full of similes drawn from pastoral life. Kings are honourably designated as " possessors of cows," gopâla ; the people meet in assembly in the cow-shed, gôsh*t*ha ;[1] the cow or bull is the centre of Hindu and Parsi sacrifice. In early Ireland the chief is rich in flocks and herds, in sheep, " and before all things in oxen."[2] " A living man," says the Hávamál of the Edda, " can always get a cow."[3] In the classic branch, one need only mention the familiar connection of *pecus* and *pecunia.*

Yet history shows us how cattle have gradually become depreciated in favour of land. Hindu and Parsi developed their house and village communities, in which the land becomes ever the real basis. In the Parsi ritual the bull of the old sacrifice is now represented only by a hair of his tail, while the author of the old Sanskrit *Aitareya Brahmana*[4] declares that all the virtue of his sacrifice is not in

---

[1] Lassen, *Indische Alterthumsk.*, i. 808, 815.
[2] Maine, *Early Hist. of Inst.*, 134.   [3] Thorpe's *Edda*, i. 43.
[4] Haug, *Ait. Brah.*, ii. 90, 91.

the cow but in the rice-cake, and tells a quaint legend of the passing of the virtue to account for his belief. Irish, Teutons, Eddic Icelanders, all have evolved the house or village community; and the same principle admittedly lies at the foundation of Greek and Roman polity.

Of other peoples, whose landmarks are not so distinct, it were wearisome to quote all. There are the Finns of the *Kalewala*, still half-nomad hunters, still tending flocks and herds, yet sowing corn around the homesteads, and sometimes enclosing the houses with a fence. There are the Amazulus, of whom Bishop Callaway has instructed us, who, along with the keeping of herds, combine the growing of corn, and have harvest festivals for the success of their crops, while yet they retain the nomad spirit in the facility with which they desert a village when it is haunted by the unpropitious wraith of some departed chieftain. *Societies of other races.*

§ 3. This likeness in social evolution between the Hebrews and the other peoples of mankind is both interesting and important. It is interesting, because it indicates that those great Hebrew institutions which have so mightily influenced the world are not the production of a special or abnormal state of society, but are the result of the orderly working of the forces of nature. It is important, because it enables us to use, for the elucidation of many passages of the Hebrew records, the analogies of similar institutions elsewhere, since likeness in *Importance of this likeness in manner of progress.*

social growth as a whole is not consistent with
aught else than likeness in the individual elements
of growth.

Such analogies we are now in a position to use.
For although the masters of sociological science
differ on many points (in what science do not
masters differ ?), yet there is now considerable unity,
not only with regard to the great periods of human
progress, but also with regard to many of what may
be termed the sub-periods of progress. And the
comparison of a general conclusion with a new
special instance serves not merely to illustrate the
instance, but to confirm, or it may well be to modify,
the general conclusion.

§ 4. A remarkable feature of social history is the
increasing definiteness, or, in Mr. Herbert Spencer's
words, the "progressive differentiation," of social
functions as civilisation progresses. Or, if we look
up, instead of down, the stream of time, the manner
in which, as we approach the recesses of antiquity,
functions which in later times are sharply marked
off from one another, gradually overlap and blend
together. This is true, not only of single functions,
but of those great groups which include the whole
of social life—the Political, Familiar,[1] and Religious.
Even in complex European civilisation, a survival of
the old blending of the political and religious functions appears in the F. D. of our coins, and of the
blending of familiar and religious in the title of the

The blend-
ing of func-
tions in early
society.

[1] I use "familiar"=*familiaris*, to indicate "belonging to the family."

Head of the Roman Church, who styles himself Papa—*Father*. But what are now mere survivals had once a living force. The "father," in many peoples of antiquity, was indistinguishable from the "chief;" the chief exercised the functions of the "priest," and the priest in turn was such because he was a "father." From this blending of function it comes that, as in Hindu literature, we shall find that matters, not only political but familiar, are enshrined in the Hebrew law-books, which are themselves the writings of priests. *Hence the origins of Hebrew society are to be sought in priestly law-books.*

We have not, however, to deal with the whole of the Hebrew juridical records. Passing by all the purely religious portion of them, our attention will be confined to the reconstruction of *Early Hebrew Life* from the political and familiar traditions, and to the consideration of the meaning of the appearance of these traditions in the Thorah.

II.—The Nomad Period.

The Nomad
Period.,
§ 5. On a lower stage of social progress than the pastoral peoples stand the nomad. By nomads I mean those tribes who exist chiefly or wholly by hunting wild animals; tribes who have only partially attained to the domestication of cattle, and to whom agriculture is hardly known. They are the "simple societies" of Mr. Herbert Spencer, the "savages" or "lower barbarians" of Mr. L. H. Morgan. Nomadism is, of course, only one of their characteristics, and is here selected as the standard because it carries on the line of thought suggested by "pastoral" and "agricultural," and also expresses the social status of Esau as compared with that of Jacob.

Descent in
the female
line a relic of
the nomad
period.
The organisation of nomad tribes is very simple and fluctuating, and leaves little traces in subsequent stages of development. One custom, however, is a notable exception to this rule. Descent is reckoned, not in the male, but in the female line; that is to say, a man's kin are the relatives of his mother, not those of his father; and all hereditary property descends in the female line.

Although sociologists differ as to the origin of the custom, there is a general agreement that maternal relationship was earlier recognised than paternal, and continued in many cases to be the legal mode

of inheritance long after paternity was fully known.[1]
And even when the two lines of descent merged, and
paternal relationship superseded maternal, special
value was attached to the latter, and the position
of women was relatively even higher than in some
more advanced forms of society. Thus, in addition
to the examples collected by the authorities mentioned in the margin, the condition of women in
Ancient India, where traditions of polyandry imply
descent in the female line, compares very favourably,
as depicted by Sir Henry Maine,[2] with that author's
account of the condition of women in Rome, where
the old tradition had died out.

§ 6. Throughout the patriarchal legends of the
Hebrews descent in the female line is an important
factor in the purity of blood. For instance, the
children of Nahor by Milcah are carefully distinguished from his children by his secondary wives.[3]
And we see in the sequel that Rebekah's descent is
practically valued as a descent from Milcah. Bethuel
disappears almost entirely; and the connection of
the families is traced entirely through the sisters
Milcah and Sarah. Isaac and Ishmael are familiar
instances of the distinction between the son of the
bond-woman and the son of the free-woman. But
even Esau's progeny are reckoned and grouped according to their various maternities.[4]

Traces in the Hebrew traditions of descent through females.

---

[1] M'Lennan, *Stud. in Anc. Hist.*, 124 ff.; Morgan, *Anc. Soc.*, 67;
Spencer, *Princip. of Sociol.*, i. 665.

[2] *Early Hist. of Inst.*, chap. xi. and pp. 310, 321.

[3] Gen. xxii. 20.　　　　[4] Gen. xxxvi. *passim.*

The same principle is implied in several of the patriarchal marriages which have already in other places been made subject of consideration. Moses' father, Amram, marries his father's sister. Nahor marries his brother's daughter. Abraham marries Sarah, "the daughter of his father, but not the daughter of his mother." This last expression is typical of the relationship between the individuals in each case; and, although quite opposed to the later Hebrew legislation, is the natural outcome of the greater relative weight attached to maternal descent.

Two also of the legends in the Book of Judges turn upon another form of the same feeling: the greater attachment between those of the same maternal blood than between those of the same paternal. Abimelech, the son of the "maid-servant" of Gideon, plots against the other sons of his father, and appeals for assistance to "the family of the house of his mother's father."[1] And he explicitly bases his claim upon his close relationship with them through his mother: "Remember also that I am your bone and your flesh." And the relevancy of the appeal is admitted in the words put into the mouth of one of Gideon's other sons: "Ye have made Abimelech king because he is your brother."[2]

In a similar manner the "sons of Gilead's wife" "thrust out" Jephthah, and decline to admit him to a share in the inheritance, because he is "the son of a strange woman,"[3] albeit of the same paternity as themselves.

[1] Judges ix. 1-3.   [2] Judges ix. 18.   [3] Judges xi. 1-3.

No doubt many, if not all, of these stories are of doubtful historicity; some are even suspected to be solar myths in disguise. But such mythological origin does not lessen their value as sociological data. The doctrine of descent which has been elicited from them is not an accidental feature of one or two isolated stories, in which it might have arisen by some casual equivoque of language, but a permanent, deep-lying feature of the entire group, expressed at times in language which, like that of Abraham, would be perfectly unintelligible if it did not correspond to some social reality.

Moreover, the early legends contain several noble types of female worth and position. Such are Debora, the prophetess; Micah's mother, the lady of her house; Jephthah's daughter, and Jael. And in the war-song of Debora, it is Sisera's *mother* who is the most eager to hear the news of the vainly hoped-for victory.

Thus the Hebrew stories have full analogies with the customs of nomad times—descent in the female line and high estimation both of maternal relationship and of women.

§ 7. But if these analogies be founded in truth, Analogies of other similar analogies may be expected in the other Semitic peoples. Semitic peoples. Exactly parallel to the stories of Abimelech and Jephthah is the famous Arab romance of Antar. Here, too, the hero, though the child of an Arab chieftain, is born of a slave-mother, and has therefore no claim to tribal rights. Once and again is he refused the hand of his nobly born cousin; and only the dire distress of his tribe compels them to turn humbly to him, like the elders of Gilead to Jephthah, and purchase the help of his mighty arm with his admittance to the rights of an Arab. And in the same romance appears, like another Debora, the stalwart lady Jaida, the chieftainess whom none but Antar could overthrow.

The cuneiform documents furnish similar evidence of the position of women in Assyria. Professor Sayce [1] adduces the old Akkadian word for "mother" —*dagal* or *damal*, signifying "mistress of the house" —as proof that in Akkad "the mother occupied the chief place in the family." A contract tablet translated by Dr. Oppert [2] shows us an Egyptian lady acting in Assyria, like Micah's mother in the Book of Judges, as "head" of her house, and purchasing in that capacity a female slave for her son. And in another contract tablet a married lady appears as part-owner of a house.[3] Our expectation is thus justified—descent in the female line, with its accompanying high respect for women, appears in two other principal branches of the Semitic race.

[1] Sayce, *Assyrian Lectures.* 153.
[2] Oppert, *Documents Juridiques,* 220 *ff.*
[3] Oppert, *ibid.,* 177 *ff.*

III.—The Pastoral Period.

§ 8. THE domestication of cattle is an epoch in The influ-ence of pas-toral life upon so-ciety. the social history of a tribe or people. It exercises a profound influence on both the physical and social life. The first has been well pointed out by Mr. Morgan ;[1] the latter is worked out in detail by Mr. Herbert Spencer.[2] Here it is necessary to draw attention to two points only — the increased definiteness of form which pastoral life gives to the family, and the community of interest which it develops among the members of the tribe.

The shepherd life tends to increased definiteness of family relationships by the facility, and even necessity, which it induces of leaving the tribe.[3] Long journeys are necessary for pasturing the cattle, assistance is necessary in tending them, and sustenance is in turn offered by the cattle themselves. Thus the individual possessor of a herd has both the means and the desire to permanently subordinate others to himself. In this way is formed a small social group in which family relationships become accurately known. Such groups are shown us in the legends of Lot and Abraham, of their separation, and of their slaves.

[1] *Anc. Soc.*, 24, 25.   [2] *Princ. Sociol.*, i. 724 *f.*   [3] *Cf.* Spencer, *ut supra.*

But the same influences which effect the isolation of the pastoral group strengthen greatly the bond of interest within the group, and produce a reciprocal interest among its members. It is the common interest to tend and protect the herds; the negligence of one member injures the whole family. And the same law holds with respect to a union of groups. Just as Lot and Abraham companied for a period together, and Jacob fed his own flocks by the side of Laban's, so now a stranger who stays long with a Bedouin tribe is expected to bear his share of the burden and heat of the day; and an Arab will marry the wife of his deceased brother so that " the family property may be kept together," and not be scattered among other families.

The mutual influence on each other of nomad and pastoral institutions.

§ 9. The natural tendency of the isolation of a pastoral group with one man as its leader is to bring paternal relationship into prominence; to supplant, in fact, descent in the female line by descent in the male line. The immediate result of this is curious.

Anomalous position of the son.

It does not at once follow that the son will inherit his father's property. On the contrary, in many societies inheritance is limited in various ways. In India the devolution of the funereal sacrifices is very different from a share in the paternal inheritance; and in Narada's *Institutes* it is distinctly said, " Six of these [the twelve kinds of sons] are kinsmen and heirs, and six are kinsmen but not heirs." [1] And there is a general limiting cause in the person

[1] Jolly, *Náradíya Dharmasástra*, p. 100.

of another heir, the brother of the deceased, who, under the more archaic system, would be the heir. Heirship of sons undoubtedly became the rule, but it is very probable that it had for a time to struggle against the older custom.

The pastoral life brought with it among the He- <small>Polygyny and its influence on the status of women.</small> brews another custom, polygyny, to use a recent but necessary coinage. Polygyny, however, results in the subordination, if not degradation, of the female sex, especially with peoples who, like the Hebrews and Arabs, had a class of secondary or slave wives. And the combination of these two factors, the degradation arising from polygyny and the surviving heirship of brothers, seems to have resulted in that inclusion of wives among heritable goods and chattels which distinguishes so many low pastoral races.[1] The custom existed among the pre-Islamite Arabs, and is adverted to in the Koran,[2] at which period it was evidently still in force. In Arabia the custom seems to have survived the introduction of the heirship of sons, and to have been only too much in accordance with the passions of the people.[3] In the Old Testament, if the Levitical prohibitions be disregarded, it occurs only as an indirect tradition. There are three instances where aspirants to the throne of Israel take the wives or concubines of the monarch as a token that they claim therewith the right to the crown. Two of

---

[1] Spencer, in *Fortnightly Rev.*, June 1877, p. 896.
[2] *Koran*, sura iv. 23; Beidhawi's *Com. in Cor.*, ed. Fleischer, i. 201.
[3] *Cf.* Muir, *Life of Mahomet*, abr. ed., 169.

these are incidents in the history of David. Once
the claim is made by Absalom during his contest
with his father;[1] and on that father's death, the
request of Adonijah for Abishag is clearly regarded
by Solomon as implying a claim to heritage of the
kingdom.[2]   The third instance is that of Abner,
whose taking of Rizpah, Saul's concubine, was viewed
with great disfavour by Ishbosheth.[3]   This case is ad-
ditionally interesting from the fact that, according to
the genealogy in 1 Sam. xiv. 50, 51, Abner was,
under the archaic rule of descent, the true heir of
Saul.

The origin of
the TRIBE.

§ 10. But the great advance which is due to pastoral
life is the birth of the *idea* of a tribe.   Aggregations
of men, more or less permanent and cohesive, existed,
of course, in earlier and lower stages of society.   But
it is pastoral life which affords the greatest facilities
for binding men together on a definite basis.   It is
a fact upon which Sir H. Maine and Von Maurer lay
great emphasis, that the Aryan race, when traced to
its earliest agricultural settlements, is found to have a
blood-organisation which greatly influenced its future
career, and only gradually yielded to the necessities of
agricultural life.   The system which is familiar to us

The tribe is
based upon
a family or-
ganisation.

from Greece and Rome, the *gens* and *curia*, the φρατρία
and δῆμος, is indeed only the legitimate development
of the original family system.   Precisely the same fact
is insisted upon by Mr. L. H. Morgan in his division of
government into an earlier "Gentile" form, based upon

[1] 2 Sam. xvi. 21.   [2] 1 Kings ii. 21 *ff.*   [3] 2 Sam. iii. 7 *ff.*

personal and racial qualifications, and characteristic of ancient society, and a later " political " form, based upon territory, and characteristic of modern society.

But the bond of relationship which existed be- *But 'family' is under-* tween the members of a *gens*, a φρατρία, a משפחה, *stood in a* must not be interpreted as we should interpret *sense.* similar terms among ourselves. Confining ourselves to Semitic peoples, it is evident, from the lax, inde- finite way in which *bên, bath; 'ibn, bint*, are used to express not only varying degrees of relationship, but also metaphorically relationship scarcely at all resembling descent, that the Hebrew or Arabic idea of a " family " must at one time have been very different to European ideas. Dr. Sprenger, for in- stance, has taken great pains to show that the Arabic genealogies of Muhammad are quite unreliable, a per- verted interpretation, in fact, of old and misunderstood traditions and ideas. And yet the very facts by which he supports his conclusion show that some real bond underlies the apparent falsehood. Some tribes, he says, call themselves the " sons " (banû), or " family " (ahl), of the chief who at the very time is ruling over them.[1] Clearly enough " banû " cannot here mean *children by blood;* and yet, if it meant nothing and indicated nothing, why did the tribe use it?

§ 11. A clue to the problem is furnished in Mr. *The explana-tion of such* Morgan's collected *Tables of the Systems of Consan-* *peculiar meaning is* *guinity and Affinity of the Races of Mankind.* Fol- *found in the*

[1] *Leben u. Lehre d. Mohammad*, iii., p. cxxxvi.

primitive
terminology
of relation-
ships.
lowing the usual linguistic divisions of race, he finds
that all systems of consanguinity fall into two
classes. One class, consisting of the Aryan and
Semite races, he terms " descriptive." These two
systems *describe*, by a special nomenclature, the
exact degree of blood relationship in which an individual stands towards each one of his ancestors and
descendants. Some of the systems are of small
extent, not extending beyond grandfather and grand-
son ; others are more extensive, and the culminating
point is reached in the Roman system, which can
accurately distinguish the degree of nearness or
remoteness of an individual with respect to any
one of his relatives within six generations back-
ward or forward.

The systems of the Turanian and other lower
races are quite different. Instead of distinguishing
five grades of remoteness, they group them together
in a remarkable manner. The brothers and sisters
of one's father, whom we call " uncles " and " aunts,"
are grouped along with the father as " parents ; "
and their children, whom we know as " cousins,"
are grouped along with one's own " brothers " and
" sisters " under one common term ; and, consis-
tently, the children of one's brother or sister, distinguished by us as " nephews " or " nieces," are
grouped along with one's own sons and daughters
as " children." Here is a typical table, the Tamil,
extracted from the larger diagram of Mr. Morgan :—

Through Father.				Through Mother.		
	Paddan, Grandfather.				Paddi, Grandmother.	
Attai, Aunt.	Takkappan, Father.	Takkappan, Father.		Tay, Mother.	Tay, Mother.	Maman, Uncle.
Maittune, Fem. Cousin.	Ego.	Annan, Elder bro. Tambi, Younger bro.		Akkarl, Elder sis. Taugay, Younger sis.	Ego.	Maittunan, Male Cousin.
Makal, Daughter.	Makan, Son.	Makan, Son.		Marumakal, Niece.	Makan, Son.	Marumakan, Nephew.
	Peran, Grandson.				Peran, Grandson.	

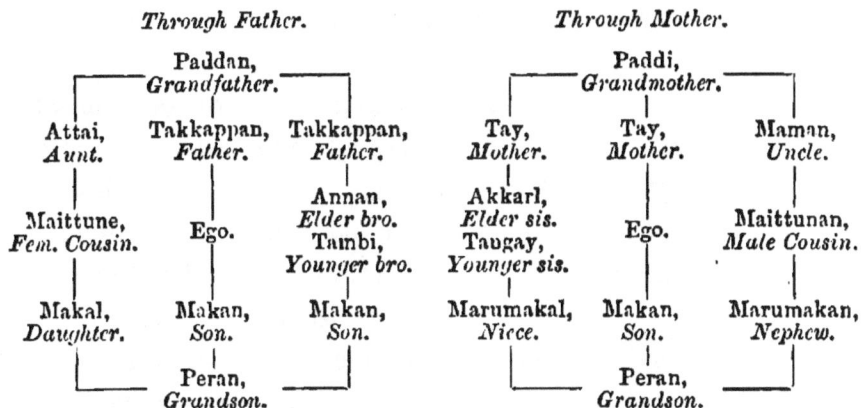

This table does not represent the system with the same pristine perfection as some tables are said to do. But sufficient is here given to show the species of classification which underlies the system. The daughter of one's grandfather is distinguished as " aunt," but all his sons are grouped as " fathers." So, too, all one's grandfather's descendants of the next generation to oneself are classed as " sons " and " daughters," and a still larger group, consisting of the fourth generation from one's grandfather and grandmother, are classed without distinction as one's " grandsons." The basis of the system is, in fact, a grouping by generations thus :—

> Grandfathers,
> Fathers,
> Brothers,
> Sons,
> Grandsons,—

the five generations who, as Ewald says, seem to be

B

the utmost that were thought of as living together at one time.

Such a system bears evident traces of its primeval character. It belongs clearly to an archaic form of society, in which, although separate families no doubt existed, none of the later needs for a definite marking-out of diverse relationships had as yet arisen. It was sufficient to define the various classes. The body of old men were the progenitors of the body of younger men, and these again of the children. Thus, without any idea of physical descent, there comes into existence between the members of a tribe a bond which has precisely the opposite effect to that of the later " descriptive " system. Kinship, instead of being dispersed, is concentrated. Kinsmen, and even non-kinsmen, who would, descriptively, be entirely separated from the family of any individual, are " classificatorily " grouped under the same appellation. That this fact afforded a solution of much that was inexplicable in the " patriarchal family " was seen by Sir Henry Maine, but he did not attempt to apply the key to the Semite or Aryan systems. This it is here proposed to do, as far as the Hebrew is concerned.

§ 12. It seems scarcely necessary to transcribe lexical passages to prove that בֵּן, אָח, אָב, all old Semite words, are frequently used in a similarly classificatory manner. אֲבוֹת אָב is a common expression for ancestor; אָח means not only a *brother*, but a *nephew*, and indeed a fellow-tribesman; בֵּן

The same terminology is used in Hebrew.

is similarly broad in signification. This usage is exactly parallel to that which has just been discussed, and it is no very bold assumption that it also is archaic. Especially does this seem to be so when we remember that in the really descriptive parts of the Semitc system (uncle, aunt, &c.), the different branches have different words, almost indicating that there had been a time when such distinctions were not needed. And we have also seen that there is independent reason to suppose that the Hebrews did pass through a period when paternity was not reckoned-of very highly.

Let us take, for example, the traditions concerning Caleb. In the earlier traditions he is known still as " Caleb, the son of Jephunneh the Kenezite." Next he appears as a chief of the tribe of Judah. Finally, in the Book of Chronicles, his foreign descent is quite lost; he becomes Caleb, the son of Hezron, the son of Judah.

And yet the two accounts, mutually contradictory, are explicable upon the " classificatory " theory, without assuming any intentional falsehood. If the tribe of Judah were in the habit of calling itself בני יהודה, " children of Judah," in the sense of " younger generation " of men over whom Judah had been, or was supposed to have been, chief, then Caleb and his house could not do otherwise, when once admitted into the tribe, than call himself by the same name. And he and the tribe would call each other אָח, " brother." Nor would there be any contradiction in so doing, for since the titles did not

represent actual blood descent, there would be no
inconsistency in being both the בֶּן of Judah and the
יֶלֶד of Jephunneh.

But when Caleb's actual descent was forgotten,
and the fortunes of his family merged into those of
the tribe of Judah, his position was indistinguishable from that of any other בֶּן יהודה; so that the
chronicler, finding traditions of his connection with
Hezron, would naturally describe Caleb as his "son,"
which indeed he was under the old nomenclature.
And, for that matter, who can say how far the
chronicler himself used his language in that archaic
sense?

It influences tradition by imparting to it a double-faced character.

§ 13. Yet, although the classificatory system takes
little heed of real family relationships, it by no
means precludes their existence. And the two
things are conjoined in the formation of a tribe.
The leader, or chief, around whom the nomad atoms
of humanity congregate, has his own blood-descen-
dants, who are within the tribe the *primi inter parcs*,
the aristocracy of the "children." To these the
chief is, of course, more even than to the rest of the
tribe. In his doings and sayings, in his memory,
his own offspring have naturally a greater interest.
And the same holds of each successive generation in
that family. So that in course of time two distinct
streams of tradition become amalgamated. One, the
tribal tradition, in which the fortunes of the tribe
are related as the fortunes of the "children of . . .;"
the other, the tradition of the fortunes of the chief

and his *real* children. And the result is that the chief looms forth in later times in a twofold aspect —personal and representative. No doubt it is hard to divide the two aspects, but they must needs exist. This, as probably the reader will recollect, is Ewald's theory, which has seemed so strange to many. Whether his restoration of the "personality" of the old Hebrew leaders is always correct may be dubious; but the doctrine has a large amount of necessary truth. It is, indeed, the true answer to Mr. Herbert Spencer's question, If these be all myth, where is the history?

IV.—The Settled or Agricultural Period.

The transition from pastoral to agricultural life. § 14. WE have now to accompany the "children of Israel" to their final settlement as an agricultural people. The transition from pastoral to agricultural life is not so much a change as a progress—a super-adding of what is new, rather than an abolition of what is old. All the characteristics of the former life remain—the tribal organisation, the common inte-rests, the wealth of cattle, the readiness to move from place to place. Only gradually are these features transformed. Little by little the tribal feeling dies away and is replaced by the sentiment of local connection; the communal interest is gradu-ally encroached upon by individuals; cattle give way to the cultivation of cereals and to commerce.

The basis of the agricul-tural settle-ment : The basis of agricultural settlement is, at least in the Aryan race, the *tribe*, of which the origin has just been discussed. To whichever branch of the race we turn, we find that underneath territorial The tribe. distinctions lies a tribal connection which is older than the territorial, and very often ignores it. In India the family organisation still survives in its primitive perfection.[1] In Rome we find the familiar division of the people into *tribes*, each of which was

---

[1] Maine, *Early Hist. of Inst.*, 78.

again divided into *curiæ* and *gentes*, which latter, it is scarcely necessary to say, are the normal group- ings of the Roman families.[1] The senate itself, by its very name, links itself with the tribal organisa- tion, in which the elders (*senes*) bear rule.[2]

In Greece there are the three Dorian tribes, who were to be found in various parts of the country;[3] the Asklepiads and Aeakids, *gentes* who were equally unconfined to one spot;[4] and in Athens tribal and territorial divisions coexisted and over- lapped each other.

In Eran, the ancient Persia, the tribal divisions into families, clans, communes, districts, were carried out with still greater consistency and uniformity.[5]

And turning to the Teutonic branch, we find that place-names in our own country record the settle- ments of tribes whose names are yet traceable upon the Continent.[6]

How such large groups arise was indicated in § 11. At the same time we saw how the pastoral life brought into prominence the actual consan- guinity within the smallest divisions of the group. Thus there coexist at the time of agricultural settle- ment two formations—the older tribal formation, based upon affinity or brotherhood, and the later family formation, which rests upon the actual blood- tie of common descent, and approaches somewhat the

And the family.

---

[1] Mommsen, *Hist. of Rome*, E. T., i. 71.   [2] *Ibid.*, i. 71.
[3] Grote, *Greece*, ii. 129.   [4] *Ibid.*, i. 152, 160.
[5] Spiegel, *Avesta*, ii. p. iv.
[6] Kemble, *Saxons in England*; Von Maurer, *Dorfverfassung*, i. 1, 2; Stubbs, *Constitutional Hist.*, i. 81.

modern family. And even in pastoral times the
tie of real consanguinity had begun to come into
collision with the tie of tribal affinity. The history
of agricultural settlement is the history of the dis-
solution of the tribe by the component families, and
of the transformation and coalescence of the families
into an entirely different political organism.

The mode of
settlement:

§ 15. If, on the one hand, it is true that "the
primitive cultivation of the land proceeded, not from
individuals, but from kindreds and tribes," it is no
less true that wherever we study these "kindreds
and tribes" they always appear split up into small
groups entirely independent of one another. It
would seem that while the necessity for communal
labour existed as strongly as in pastoral life, the
size of the group within which that communism
could exist was greatly decreased. It was no longer
possible for a whole tribe to live together in joint
cultivation of a huge territory; it was needful that
the tribe should split into smaller sections, each of
which should cultivate a smaller tract. This simple
and obvious necessity of agricultural life was fraught
with great consequences. First, however, let us see
how the division of the great tribes was carried out.

Division of
the tribe into
small groups.

How carried
out by the
Aryan race.

The common Aryan expression for the earliest
form of settlement appears in the Sansk. *vis*, the
Lith. *wies* (in wies-pati), Greek οἶκος, Lat. *vicus*.[1]
This institution, as the divergent meanings of its
variant forms show, was intermediate between the

[1] Lassen, *Indische Alterthumskunde*, i. 796.

simple "house" and the developed "town."[1] It
consisted, apparently, of a cluster of houses (containing about five families) located around the
cattle-fold, and forming a small village, or "high
street."[2] It still lingers on in India as the "Joint
Undivided Family" of Sir Henry Maine. In such
a family the members unite in undivided worship,
take their meals at the same board, and hand down
their property undivided from one generation to
another. Constantly engaged in the cultivation of
land, it is nevertheless " only accidentally connected
with it. . . . What holds it together is not land but
consanguinity."[3] Traces of this primitive society
appear also in the family rites of the Romans, and
in the "syssitia" of the Spartans, though these
belong rather, in the form in which tradition has
preserved them, to the next stage of development.

Here, therefore, the great pastoral tribe is seen
splitting up into its component "families," whic
form that "house" which language shows to be the
basis of the "village" and "town."

The next stage is known as the "House Community," and is the natural development of it. "It
is simply the joint family of the Hindus, allowed
to expand itself without hindrance and settled for
ages on the land." "The community is a community of kinsmen, but though the common an-
cestry is probably to a great extent real, the
tradition has become weak enough to admit of

*Develop-
ment of the
groups into
house com-
munities.*

[1] Pott, *Wurzel-Wörterbuch*, i. 231.   [2] Lassen, *ut supra*, i. 797.
[3] Maine, *Early Hist. of Inst.*, 79

considerable artificiality being introduced into the association . . . through the adoption of strangers from outside. Meantime the land tends to become the true basis of the group; it is recognised as of pre-eminent importance to its vitality; and it remains common property, while private ownership is allowed to show itself in moveables and cattle."[1] Such house communities are found in Dalmatia, Illyria, and Sclavonia. Teutonic joint-families have left their names in Uppingham and Gillingham. The institution, indeed, is almost universal in this stage. Even the Iroquois Indians lived in large houses, each of which accommodated twenty families, with a separate hearth to every twain of them.[2]

§ 16. That the Semitic race followed a parallel course of development there is abundant evidence. Ewald has noted the similarity between the Hebrew division into " tribes " and " families," and the classic division into gentes and δῆμοι.[3] So, too, Movers has shown that in Phœnicia the great tribe, שבט, rested finally upon the בית אבות, analogous to the φυλή and πάτραι of Greece.[4] The Hebrew traditions distinctly assert the allotment of the land to have been by families.

Of the house community itself there are traces both in Assyria and Judea. In Assyrian, *alu,*

Parallel de-velopment of the Semitic race.

The house community in Assyria.

---

[1] Maine, *Early Hist. of Inst.*, 80, 81.
[2] Morgan, *Systems of Consang.*, 153, *n.* ; *cf.* with his *Anc. Soc.*, 75.
[3] *Alterthümer d. V. Israel*, 319.
[4] Movers, *Die Phönizier*, ii. (i.) 480 *f.*

meaning "town," is identical with the Heb. אהל
and the Arab. *'ahl.*[1] Passing from " tent," through
" family," into " people," and finally into " town," it
is strikingly analogous to the Sansk. *vis.* And as a
matter of detail it is curious to note that Assyria,
preserving the record of tent-life and also actual
family life in its great cities, is in exactly the same
position as Eran among the Aryans, which, while
preserving the family organisation the most perfectly (§ 14), preserves also the record that the race
once lived in tents.[2]

The Assyrian house community is preserved in
two contract-tablets, translated into Latin, French,
and English by Dr. Oppert.[3] The translations are
still very uncertain in many places, but the facts I
am about to quote seem to be reliable. One tablet
records the alienation by one Sirusur, son of Killi,
of a portion of his property as a dowry for his
daughter. The domains of the " house of Killi"
(bit Killim) are extensive. Clauses in the tablet
provide against a reclamation at any future time
by any of the " house of Killi," and among such
possible claimants are noted (I quote from Dr.
Oppert's literal Latin version[4]) : " Fratres, filii,
familia, viri et mulieres, famuli et ancillæ domus
Killi, seu alienus, seu hospes, et seu quisquis
is erit."

A second tablet recounts the grant to a courtier
of a portion of the domains of the " house of Ada."

[1] Sayce, *Assyrian Lects.*, 144. [2] Spiegel, *Avesta*, i. 140, *n.* 2.
[3] *Documents Juridiques de l'Assyrie*, 85 *ff.* [4] *Ibid.*, 88.

This house, too, was a great corporation possessed
of extensive lands, bounded by the estates of other
great "houses." It has a complete organisation of
officers to deal with its internal management, each
of whom is designated as a functionary "of the
house of Ada." And the "house" itself is said in
the tablet to be composed of "fratres, filii, propinqui, propinqui familiæ." It would seem, too, to
have been a corporation of long standing, for the
ruler, or "master," is not mentioned by name, but
only by his office. And Dr. Oppert, after noticing
the privileges of the "house," adds, "Nous remar-
quons particulièrement une menace pour celui qui
nierait le droit du souverain, et contesterait la trans-
mission du pouvoir au satrape dela maison d' Ada.
Ce qui suppose que le terrain concédé faisait partie
d'un domaine considérable."[1]

In Israel there are several relics of this kind
of community. In the Book of Judges we read
of the "house" of Micah. This is incidentally
mentioned to consist of "houses near to Micah's
house." Its head is a woman, Micah's mother. It
has its own chapel, priest, and vestments, and can
upon occasion muster a goodly array of fighting
men.[2] Movers sees traces of the family-worship in
the common sacrifice-feast of Samuel's town, and in
Adonijah's feast in 1 Kings i. 9. And the whole
organisation comes out clearly in the excuse made
by David for his absence from Saul's table:[3] "Our
family hath a sacrifice" ("a yearly sacrifice for all

---

[1] *Doc. Juridiques*, 115.   [2] Judges xvii., xviii., *passim.*
[3] 1 Sam. xx. 29.

the family," ver. 6) in the city; and my brother, he
hath commanded me to be there." Here the family
is seen not only to be united in property and worship, but also to exercise a certain authority over
members at a distance.

So far, therefore, the Hebrews have followed the
same order of progress as other societies. In the
house community the isolation induced by agricultural life is beginning to weaken the old tribal
feeling. Although the actual consanguinity of many
members of the community is undoubted, there is no
corresponding feeling of brotherhood. The house, as
we saw in the "house of Ada," instead of being a
portion of a larger organism, has itself swelled into
a developed organism.

§ 17. The gradual decadence of the tribal tie leaves
contiguity of habitation, "neighbourhood," as the
only possible bond between the members of a
village. The persons are the descendants of the
old house community, but the idea of consanguinity
has died, and their relations to each other begin to
be based upon the fact that they all derive their
subsistence from the same tract of land. And thus
are evolved numerous regulations for the social welfare of the community, which fall into three groups
—right of homestead; rights and duties as respects
the land; rights and duties as respects the fellow-
villagers.

The decadence of the house community originates a new bond of union.

The homesteads appertain to each family, which
sometimes consists of several households. The

The village community.

houses occupy the position of the primitive group,
in the centre of the village lands. Very often the
village is surrounded with a fence; then the houses
form the nucleus of the future "zaun" or "town."
The householders, representing the "elders" or
"fathers" of earlier days, form the village council.[1]

Round the homesteads the land for a considerable
space is cultivated. Here are the cornfields, vineyards, orchards of the village. This space is the
"suburbs" of the later town.[2]

Beyond the cultivated portion—the "arable mark,"
as Teutonic nomenclature terms it—extends the
common pasture land, whereon each villager may
graze his cattle.[3] The pasture land is bounded by
the uncleared space, the wood, and very often by a
rivulet which supplies the village with water.[4] Beyond the wood extends the unreclaimed waste land,
the property of the whole tribe or people, and
encroached upon by one or another of the various
communities as occasion requires.

Tenure of vil-
lage lands.

Individual ownership of land is not recognised.
In the typical village communities of Germany the
land is the property of the village as a corporate
body. Individuals only acquire the use of a certain portion for a limited period.[5] In India and
other countries the land is divided within the village
into family districts, but even here the rule is main-

[1] Maine, *Village Communities*, 78; Von Maurer, *Geschichte d. Dorfverfassung*, i. 30, 31.

[2] Maine, *ut supra*, 79; Von Maurer, *ut supra*, i. 33, 34.

[3] Von Maurer, *ut supra*, 40, 41.   [4] *Ibid.*, 47.

[5] Maine, *ut supra*, 76, 77, *ff.*; Von Maurer, *ut supra*, i. 33, *ff.*;
Stubbs, *Const. Hist.*, i. 51, 65.

tained that individual ownership is not recognised. Each family or household has allotted to it a strip of the arable land, and possesses the rights of grazing cattle, drawing water, and hewing wood in the pasture lands, river, and wood. But at the end of a certain period—three, five, or seven years—the arable land is again cast into one common lot, and a new division is made, giving each household a strip equal in extent, but different in situation, to the former strip, and so dividing equally the use of fertile and sterile land among the villagers.

The same principle of common interest which existed in pastoral and early agricultural times among members of the tribe and family is applied to village life. In all things the villager must consider the rights of his fellows. He may not sully the river, nor wantonly cut down wood. What is lost or strayed he must faithfully return. He must assist his fellows whenever called upon to do so: in reaping; in building or repairing homesteads or roads; in conveying loads; even in family matters. In cultivating his own allotment he must conform to the village rules of fallow, rotation of crops, and the like, " minute and multifarious rules which have for their object to reconcile a common plan and order of cultivation on the part of the whole brotherhood with the holding of distinct lots in the arable land by separate families." [1]

Such, in broad outline, is the village community,

Reciprocal rights and duties of the villagers.

---

[1] Maine, *Village Communities*, chaps. iii., iv.; Von Maurer, *Dorfverfassung*, i., divisions ii., iv., v.

the normal development of the agricultural period; such therefore is the standard to which the Hebrew development may be expected to conform. Few, however, even in Aryan lands, conform entirely to to the ideal standard; each community has its individual points of divergence. We shall therefore be prepared to find that the Hebrew also has a sub-type of its own.

§ 18. But before comparing the normal village community with Hebrew traditions, attention must be called to an important difference. Hitherto no mention has been made, except incidentally, of religion. A national religion in such unformed societies is scarcely conceivable. And so far as religion influenced early social formations, it seems to have been a kind of constant factor; its effects are everywhere much the same. But in considering the village communities of Aryan races, one perceives that their primitive religions have been modified or completely changed. The Teutonic communities completed their development under the influence of Christianity, which supplanted the old Northern creeds. The old Roman religion was greatly leavened with Greek culture, and the Greek religion itself, notwithstanding its influence upon the people, does not appear to have possessed any visible political unity. The deities seem to have had nothing which could weld them into one great power influencing the whole race as one man. And hence we find that in Greece, as in Rome and Ger-

Note (left margin): Divergent influence, in Israel and Arya, of religion:

Note (left margin): (i.) In Aryan communities;

many, the influence of the land became paramount. The people were split up into "towns," each forming a little commonwealth, jealous to the utmost of its own independence, and lacking any feeling of community with cities at a little distance; and when a new union was brought about, it was on the basis, not of kinships, but of townships.

But in Israel it was not so. At the outset the (ii.) In Israel. tribes undoubtedly hung together very loosely. They seldom hesitated to war one upon another. The struggles with the Philistines were entirely local; seldom, if ever, until David's time, did all Israel as Exclusive- a nation fight a pitched battle. And so little did tribes: even the genius of David and the magnificence of Solomon weld the tribes together, that immediately upon the death of the latter monarch they split into two empires. And probably Israel would have fallen entirely into the dislocated state of Greece Checked by the influence but for the conservative influence of Yahwism. For of religion, the worship of Yahweh was inseparable from the idea of kinship with Abraham. It was through kinship with him that the Hebrew gained that peculiar favour with which he believed his God had blessed him. This, the fundamental idea of Judaism, goes back undoubtedly into very early times, prior certainly to the settlement in Canaan; but it gained great force from the peculiar posi- Which was tion of the priesthood. Present in every tribe and the position of the priest. village, and yet cut off from participation in the tribal quarrels of other Israelites, their whole interest lay in maintaining the worship of the God

C

of "Abraham, Isaac, and Jacob," and thus they
were to the people a living memorial of the great
forefathers of the nation. The old tradition was
clothed with all the authority that a Christian
doctrine receives from being "quod semper, quod
ubique, quod ab omnibus." This priestly influence
did not prevent individuals or tribes from considering their own material interests; but it had the
effect of making all, tribes as well as individuals,
jealous to preserve the particular thread which
bound themselves to the Patriarchs. A man of
Judah was careful to preserve the tradition of his
family within the tribe, and the tribe as a body
was equally careful to maintain its position in the
genealogies of Jacob's sons. And this assisted very
powerfully in keeping alive the old groups of the
pastoral period. The tribes, as tradition tells us
(and the tradition accords with other records of
similar settlements), settled down by tribes and
families in distinct sections; the allotment being,
in a broad way, marked out by the chief, and each
tribe giving its component "gentes" a fixed allotment within its district. In other lands this mode
of settlement was extinguished by the circumstances
of agricultural life, and the old family names soon
ceased to correspond to any living reality. But as
Yahwism continued powerful in Israel (or rather,
increased in power), the necessity also remained for
keeping up the connection between each Israelite
and Abraham. And as this was shown in the tribe
by the fixed district in the land of Israel, so it was

requisite for the "gentes" (משפחות) to have their
fixed allotment within the tribal land. And this
feeling is apparent in the pains with which the
writers of Joshua and Chronicles record the traditional allotments and family divisions.

§ 19. It was remarked in § 14 that the old tribal
bond was dissolved by agricultural settlement. In
Hebrew history it is more strictly correct to say
that the tribal idea was absorbed by the "familiar"
idea.

The evolu-
tion of the
agricultural
form.

It will be recollected that the family of actual
consanguinity already existed in pastoral times
within the *gens*. When the tribe was settled upon
the land, and these smaller families became the
agricultural unit, it is obvious that through the
family primarily a man must trace his connection
with the tribe. But he has also through his *gens*
another connection with similar families. Thus the
gentes, though themselves connected only by figura-
tive kinship, tend each to consist of groups internally
connected by actual kinship. And as the smaller
families are continually dying out, diminishing, or
increasing, cases like that of Zelophehad, who had
no sons but only daughters, will continually arise,
and the *gens* will tend more and more to consist
of persons who are actually all more or less nearly
akin to each other. Such a tendency in the house
community has already been noted in a quotation
from Sir Henry Maine. He adds, that while the
fact grows stronger the *tie* grows weaker. We see

the reason why this was not so in Israel.   The
Hebrew settlement took this form: several families,
actually blood relatives, occupy one district, and
form the *gens*, מִשְׁפָּחָה; several such מִשְׁפָּחוֹת hold
adjoining districts, and together form the "tribe,"
the old "brotherhood."   Thus the two ideas blend
together: but for the tribal bond the people would
not have settled on contiguous lands; the settlement
on tribal land becomes in turn evidence of connection with the tribe, and the grasp both of the land
and the tribe is strengthened by the actual kinship
between men of the same *gens*.   The result of this
interaction of ideas was the fusion of the family
and the village.   "Neighbour" and "brother" are
interchangeable terms for a fellow-Israelite.   The
return of an Israelite to his village was designated
by the Hebrew writers as a return to his family, to
the inheritance of his fathers.

Thus we have an explanation of the fact, otherwise
so curious, that the genealogies of the chronicler,
while purporting to be genealogies of persons, appear
to be really records of the relations of towns.   We
have seen already that the expression "son" bears a
different meaning from its modern use; we see now
that a town and a *gens*, a מִשְׁפָּחָה, were actually
conterminous.   There is nothing strange in this;
Syracuse and Locri, Uffington and Gillingham, are
relics of the same stage in Arya; among the Hebrews
the development was less complex, and the survivals
are consequently more numerous.

While, therefore, we compare the Hebrew laws

with those of other village communities, because
these are the normal product of agricultural life,
we shall find the earlier formations still moulding
functions whereon their influence in other societies
has been entirely obliterated.

§ 20. In comparing the Hebrew with Aryan and
other communities, it will be well to take the points
of contact in this order : land, government, reciprocal
rights and duties, survivals.

The Hebrew village community.

The houses of the village do not require much
consideration. We have seen already (§ 16) that the
Hebrews formed house communities, which form the
basis of the village community. We pass, therefore,
to the village lands.

1. The village lands.

In 1 Chron. vi. 55, 56 (Heb. 40, 41) it is written,
"They gave them [the Levites] Hebron in the land
of Judah, and the suburbs thereof (מִגְרָשֶׁיהָ) round
about it. But the fields of the city (שְׂדֵה הָעִיר), and
the villages thereof, they gave to Caleb, the son of
Jephunneh."

What were the "suburbs" and the "fields," the
מגרש and the שדה ?

The מגרש is mentioned throughout 1 Chron. vi.
as the ordinary appendage of a town. In Num.
xxxv. it is defined as a space of two thousand cubits
round the town, available for cattle, and "goods,"
and beasts, partly therefore for pasture. But it is
also used as synonymous with "fruit:" to plunder
the מגרש is to plunder a town of its produce. Here,
therefore, the מגרש would be a cultivated tract.

The suburbs.

The שדה, which is so evidently contrasted with the מגרש in 1 Chron. vi., borders upon the meaning of the latter word so far as sometimes to mean a cultivated tract; but it is very often used in a context which opposes it to cultivated land. "Wild beasts" are חית השד. The man, in the story of Elijah, who goes out to gather potherbs, gathers by mistake גפן שדה, the grapes of a "wild vine." And the law that when a man is found slain in the שדה,[1] measurement shall be made to the nearest town, indicates that the שדה extended a considerable distance from the town, up to the שדה indeed of the adjoining town. There thus appears to be a fairly marked distinction between the two words; the מגרש being the cultivated belt round a town, the שדה a broader tract not necessarily under cultivation.

In substance the same distinction is drawn by Von Maurer between the "arable" and "pasture" marks of the German communities. "To each householder in the village," he says, "there belonged from the first a definite allotment of fields, meadows, vineyards, &c., in the field mark ('arable mark'), and an ideal share in the user (*Nutzungen, utilitates*) of the common forests and meadows, of water, of roads and paths, and of everything necessary for agriculture. That is, the mark of a village was usually, so far as it was *adapted for cultivation* (terra arabilis, aratoria), *and lay around the village,* divided among the body of communists; but so far

[1] Deut. xxi. 1 *ff.*

as it was *less adapted to cultivation,* or lay *more distant from the village,* left in undivided commonalty."[1] Without going so far as to suggest that מגרש and שדה should always be rendered "arable" and "pasture" mark respectively, I think it may be fairly assumed that they do, as a rule, correspond to the definition of the marks as given by Von Maurer. This receives confirmation from the identical position which the wood holds in both The wood. communities. It, too, was the common property of the Hebrew villagers, as appears incidentally in Deut. xix. 5, "When a man goeth into the wood with his *neighbour* to hew wood," which is exactly parallel to the German laws which enforce the cutting down of wood by the *whole body* of villagers at stated seasons. Kirjath-jearim, "the city of the woods," on the borders of Judah and Benjamin, indicates by its name that the wood formed the boundary of those tribes. And in 2 Kings vi. 1–6, we see the actual formation of a new village. The sons of the prophets go out from their old village towards Jordan, and, taking wood from the forest, make them a place "*there,*" that is, clearing a space in the free forest, exactly as Teutonic youths would have done.

§ 21. As rulers of the village we find in the Pentateuch two orders of persons—the "elders" (זקנים) and the "judges" (שפטים). The judges will

ii. The village officers:
1. Elders and judges.

---

[1] Von Maurer, *Dorfverfassung,* i. 33, 34; *Cf.* Maine, *Vill. Comm.,* 78–80.

require consideration in a future section. Of the "elders" it is unnecessary to say much. They are universally recognised as the representatives of the old tribal council, and are exactly parallel to the elders of an Aryan community.

2. The priest　But I incline to think that another village functionary appears in the Pentateuch, viz., the priest, or Levite. In addition to the council of elders, **Is found in other communities:** village communities possess, almost necessarily, various officers to guard the various interests of the community and to perform for it various services.[1] Among these the priest holds a high position, and, indeed, succeeds in most cases in acquiring considerable rights. In Israel the Levite admittedly dwelt in the country, and was not **His position in Israel;** always attached to the temple at Jerusalem. He has no share in the communal lands, though he dwells "within the gates" of the village; he is classed along with the fatherless, the poor, and the widow as an object of communal care. Like them, he is fed by tithes; but, unlike them, he is a person of consideration, as we glean from the desire which both Micah and the tribe of Dan showed to possess a Levite as their official organ of worship. In Deuteronomy the priest appears along with the "elders" or "judges" as a judicial functionary. In chap. xix. 17 the "priests and judges," in chap. xvii. 9, "the priests and the judge" are mentioned together. In chap. xxi.,

---

[1] Lists of such officers are found in Maine, *Vill. Comm.*, 125; *Asiat. Soc. Journ.*, i. 298; Von Maurer, *Dorfverfassung*, ii. 95 *ff.*

where the representatives of two villages, on whose
borders a man has been slain, meet to deprecate
the wrath of Yahweh, the prayer for averting the
guilt of murder is placed in the lips of the " priests,
the sons of Levi." Finally, in apparent contradiction to what has just been said, the Levite often
acquired a patrimony in his village. All these
curious attributes are those of a village officer.
Not being a member of the tribe, he has no share
in the tribal land. As a recompense for his services
he is paid in kind, the only money in existence in
those days.[1] Of the importance which he tends to
acquire a remarkable illustration is given by those
village accountants in India whom our Government
in the days of yore erroneously supposed to be
owners instead of servants of the village.[2] And the
priest's acquisition of personal property in land is
only one form of the " benefice " which is well known
to be one of the earliest instances of individual
ownership within the mark.[3] We shall therefore
do no violence to Hebrew tradition by assuming the
priest to have been a village functionary. As we
proceed there will meet us further indirect con-
firmations of this assumption.

Analogous to that of a village officer.

§ 22. Passing to the rights and duties of the
villagers one towards another, there are numerous
points of agreement between the Pentateuchal legislation and the traditional rules of village com-

iii. Recipro-cal rights and duties of the villagers:

[1] *Cf.* Maine, *Ancient Law*, 268, for a similar custom in Servia.
[2] *Cf.* Maine, *Vill. Comm.*, 125, and Von Maurer, *ut supra.*
[3] Maine, *Vill. Comm.*, 132 ; Hallam, *Middle Ages*, chap. vii.

munities. Many of the Hebrew laws are such as must necessarily be framed in any society, such as those against theft, murder, adultery, damage by cattle, and the like. These need no explanation, and are not specially traceable (except in some points of detail) to the communal stage of existence. But there are others, of which some have become obsolete and some have received esoterical explanations, and these others it is which give the Pentateuch the strange and unreal aspect it wears in modern eyes. These laws, I hope to show, are distinctly referable to the village community.

Their two-fold aspect in Israel.

Here the form of the Hebrew laws is controlled by that fusion of the family and the village which was dwelt upon in § 19. In the Hindu law-books, drawn up for the guidance of the individual during his whole life, both family and community appear as aspects of individual life. In Rome family regulations, under the technical title of *patria potestas*, have separated from the communal into a distinct branch of judicature. In Germany some family regulations were merged into those of the communal. All these divergences arise out of divergent social environments. The Hebrew is different from all. In it both family and communal regulations form parts of a legislature appertaining to a social aggregate possessing both a "familiar" and a communal aspect. We will deal with the aspects separately; first, that of the family, and then that of the commune.

§ 23. The legislation in Deut. xxii. 13–21, relative

to a wife who is wrongfully accused of incontinence,
and to a wife who is rightly so accused, is paralleled
by the Hindu legislation in *Nárada*, xii. 34, 35, and
31, 36. The first passages run thus : " 34. If a man,
actuated by hatred, says of a girl, ' She is no maid,'
he is to be fined a hundred *panas* if he cannot prove
her shame. 35. If a man abandons a girl without
defects after he has chosen her, he is to be punished,
and must marry the girl even against his will." The
passages 31, 36, bear a similar analogy to Deut.
xxii. 20, 21.

Exactly the same laws are found in *Yajnavalkya*,
i. 66; *Manu*, viii. 224, 225.

So, too, the law in Deut. xxiv. 5, " When a man
hath taken a new wife, he shall not go out to war,
neither shall he be charged with any business; but
he shall be free at home one year, and shall cheer
up his wife which he hath taken," is aptly paralleled
in Germany. " Reciprocal aid and succour," says
Von Maurer, " extended even to marital duties."
After an illustration corresponding to the Hindu
levirate, he proceeds, " Altogether, there seems to
have been great respect for marital duties. For
the peasant-right of Wendhagen says, ' Wann ein
Ehemann nebst seiner Frau sein Guth besehen
wollte, und bekähme eine Lust bey ihr zu schlaffen,
käme aber einer mit Fuder Heuf drauf zugefahren,
wie sich der verhalten ? Wenn einer drauf zufahren
kommt, so soll er stille halten, und die Zwille
untersetzen, bis solches vollendet, wann er es aber
nicht abwarten kann, so soll er weit umhin fahren,

als man ein Pferd absehen kann, auf dasz solches nicht verhindert würde.' "[1] Which remarkable law is sufficiently explicit for us to dispense with any further observations on the matter.

ii. Paternal power.

In the law relative to the stubborn son in Deut. xxi. 18–21, we meet one phase of what in Roman law was an important branch of jurisprudence. "The parent had over his child the *jus vitæ necisque*, and *a fortiori* of uncontrolled personal punishment; he can modify their personal condition at pleasure; he can give a wife to his son; he can give his daughter in marriage, . . . and he can sell them."[2] This *potestas* is a relic of the old patriarchal power, of the rise and fall whereof Sir Henry Maine elsewhere gives a vivid account.[3] In Rome it is severed from the communal law; in Israel, on the contrary, it has grown into a part of that law.

iii. Reverence to old age.

Yet once more let us turn to India. There, among the duties enjoined on the student, we find that reverence to parents and elders which so often meets us in the Pentateuch. The Hebrew law takes cognisance of smiting one's father and mother (Exod. xxi. 15); cursing father or mother (Exod. xxi. 17); fearing father and mother (Lev. xix. 1); setting light by them (Deut. xxvii. 16); of cursing the deaf, and putting a stumblingblock before the blind (Lev. xix. 14); or turning the blind out of the way (Deut. xxvii. 18); honouring the face of the old man (Lev.

---

[1] Von Maurer, *ut supra*, i. 339.   [2] Maine, *Ancient Law*, 138.
[3] *Early Hist. Inst.*, 116 *f.*

xix. 32); and finally, to include all instances here, reviling God (אלהים) and cursing the ruler of the people (Exod. xxii. 28). Prohibitions against cursing and enchantments are laid down, with their due punishments, in *Manu*, viii. 274, 275, and *Yajna-valkya*, ii. 204–211, with much greater detail than the Hebrew. All the law-books have an injunction to make way on the road for an old man, a sick one, or a woman.[1] Cursing the gods (here, without doubt, deities) and the king is prohibited in *Âpas-tamba* (i. 11, 31) and *Manu* (iv. 163).

§ 24. Passing to the second or communal aspect of the Hebrew community, we meet at once that notable mark of the village community, the *wergild*, or joint responsibility for murder. The Hebrew law runs thus: " If one be found slain in the land which Yahweh thy God giveth thee to possess it, lying in the field, and it be not known who hath slain him, then thy elders and thy judges shall come forth, and they shall measure unto the cities which are round about him that is slain; and it shall be, that the city which is next unto the slain man, even the elders of that city shall take an heifer," &c.

In England " the maegth share in the wergild paid for their slain brother, and contribute to the payment for one whom their brother has slain." [2] In Germany the same responsibility was general. The communities had to answer for the murders com-

[margin note: The communal aspect. i. Wergild.]

---

[1] Âpastamba, ii. 5, 11, in *Sacred Books of the East*, ii., and the references there given.

[2] Stubbs, *Const. Hist.*, i. 82.

mitted in their mark, and probably also for other crimes.[1]

The Hindu law approaches even more nearly to the Hebrew. "271. If a murder or a theft take place, the guilt shall fall upon the overseer (aufseher) of the place (ort) if the track [I presume of the murderer or the thief] do not lead beyond the place; if the crime take place upon the highroad, the guilt falls upon the overseer of the district of the place (ortsgebiet), but upon the constable if it take place at any other spot within the district.

"272. That place shall be answerable within whose boundary the crime has been committed or whither the track leads; or five places, if it was committed a krośa beyond the bounds, or even ten places."[2]

ii. Strayed cattle.

Removal of landmarks is too evidently an universal law to need quotation; but the law, "Thou shalt not see thy brother's ox or his sheep go astray, and hide thyself from them: thou shalt in any case bring them again unto thy brother," is well illustrated by this, "If one see his neighbour's cattle come to harm, how should he act that such cattle may be saved? He must let his own work alone, be it as urgent as it will, and do by the cattle as he would have it done to his" (wie er es selbst gern wollte).[3]

In this context, too, it may be permitted to suggest that possibly the words of Christ, "Whoso-

---

[1] Von Maurer, i. 350, 351, where numerous instances are given.
[2] Stenzler's *Yajnavalkya.*   [3] Von Maurer, *Dorfverfassung,* i. 337.

ever shall compel thee to go a mile, go with him twain," may receive light from this: "Whenever a villager would travel, either by horse or on foot, and cannot get home, his neighbours shall come to help him, *five miles on horseback and three on foot.*" [1]

Two other curious laws are also referable to this period of communal life, viz., the law against hewing down fruit trees, and the law concerning bird's nests.

The Hebrew law respecting fruit trees is paralleled both in Germany and India; the Hindu law coinciding remarkably with the Hebrew in giving the same reason for the prohibition. iii. Fruit trees.

"When thou shalt besiege a city a long time in making war against it to take it, thou shalt not destroy the trees thereof by forcing an axe against them; for thou mayest eat of them, and thou shalt not cut them down, . . . only the trees which thou knowest that they be not trees for meat, thou shalt destroy and cut them down." [2]

The German communities forbad the undue hewing down of trees: "Das niemand kein eisendrudel oder aichen reifstangen gross oder klein in der allment hawen soll." "Derselben Holtz Sleg verschonen, dass das jung Holtz seins gewächs nit verhindert werde." [3]

The planting of fruit trees was incumbent on many villages, and many curious customs arose thereout.[4]

---

[1] Von Maurer, *Dorfverfassung*. i. 337.   [2] Deut. xx. 19, 20.
[3] Maurer, *Dorfcerfassung*, i. 242, 243.   [4] Von Maurer, i. 287, 283.

The Hindu laws present a closer parallel to the Hebrew :—

"227. For hewing off the branches, stems, and for the total destruction of trees whose branches grow again, *or of such as afford a support of life*, is enforced a penalty doubling itself from twenty pañas upward.

"228. For trees which grow in a graveyard, a churchyard, a boundary, a consecrated place, or stand near a temple, is enforced a double penalty, and similarly for notable trees."[1]

The enactment appears also in *Manu*, viii. 285, and is implied in *Nárada*, ii. 31, p. 36, where "one who is carrying an axe is a destroyer of trees" is mentioned among the "evident signs" of crime which render "witnesses superfluous."

iv. Birds'-nesting. The restriction in Deut. xxii. 6, 7, against taking an old bird along with the young, rests upon the idea that one may have "right of user" in the bird to the extent of sharing in its produce; but one may not claim entire possession of it. Birds and bees are mentioned together in old German law; and the folk-law of Bayern, after regulating the use of bees, continues in these interesting words, " Pari modo de avibus sententia subjacetur, ut nullus de alterius silva aves tollere præsumet, nisi ejus commarcanus (*i.e.*, fellow-communist) fuit."[2] Here the Hebrew has decidedly the more correct form.

v. Refreshment of travellers. The restrictions in Deut. xxiii. 24, 25, upon the use to be made of a neighbour's vines or corn

---

[1] Stenzler, *Yajnavalkya.*   [2] Von Maurer, i. 277, 278.

are also paralleled in Germany, where travellers
may *pluck* and *eat*, but may not carry away.[1]

Finally, the sanitary regulation in the same chap. vi. Personal
cleanliness.
v. 13, 14, meets its fellow in India, where the law
is given in much greater detail.[2]

§ 25. We have now traced the fundamental unity Transition to
survivals.
of type between the Hebrew and other village communities, and we have also observed the particular
development of Hebrew life which produced the
peculiar features of the chronicler's genealogies—
families which are also towns and trade guilds which
are also families. In all the illustrations we have
examined we have seen the community in the full
vigour of life; the laws which have been discussed
are the laws of a living society. We have now to
pass to survivals of the community, laws no longer
of a living society, but based upon the usages of one
that has passed away. But to do this we must first Preliminary
considera-
consider two elements which helped to modify the tions.
survivals into their present shape. These elements
are the Goel and the Shofetim.

§ 26. Even at this comparatively early stage of The Goel
social life the Goel in Hebrew history is himself a
survival. In patriarchal life the "next of kin" is
an important personage. To him the tribe looks to His importance in pas-
avenge a kinsman's death or misfortune; on him the toral times.
widow and fatherless depend for support; he it is
who inherits the property of the deceased in default

---

[1] Von Maurer, i. 331–333.   [2] Âpastamba, i. 11, 30.

of direct heirs—if indeed he be not, under the archaic system, the heir himself; he, when the heir is young, manages for him such property as he may possess. After the transition to agricultural life various causes combine to bring about the decadence of this importance. The avenging of blood is superseded by the police regulations of the commune; the widow and fatherless become the care of the commune; and the control of the heir's property passes into simple trusteeship. And then as, little by little, the patriarchal bond is loosened, and members of one family scatter hither and thither, the "next of kin" merges into the "relative," with no more claim or interest in his family than perhaps a score of others. But in Israel it was not so. There, where the worship of Yahweh kept the descent from Abraham fresh in the minds of the people, the family type coexisted, as we have just seen, with the communal, and coalesced with it. And accordingly the functions of elder and Goel were very often united in the same person; nay, the functions of the Goel tended to expand into conterminity with those of the elder. For if a villager were slain in a town like Gilead, in which the family tradition was especially strong, the strict right of blood revenge would cease with kin of the fifth generation. But an elder of the town beyond the fifth degree would feel equally with one within it the loss sustained from the communal point of view by the death of the villager, and would be equally ready to avenge it. That is to say, that in his function as an elder he would usurp a function which as

Goel did not strictly belong to him. Exactly the same may be said with respect to the maintenance of widows and orphans, and with respect to redemption from debt and slavery. Thus we have at once an explanation of the plural form גֹּאֲלִים in Ruth ii. 20. Albeit the nomad can have but one Goel, yet in a village community any elder would feel himself bound to exercise the same functions.

Three duties of the Goel still exist in the Hebrew law-books, viz., the duties of avenging blood, of raising up seed to a kinsman, and of redeeming the forfeited share of a kinsman in the common land. The last of these functions must be deferred until the consideration of pure survivals; the other two we may fitly dwell upon here. *Survivals of his duties.*

The avenging of blood will not need much explanation. It is a well-known feature of nomad pastoral life which survives in the arrangements of the village community.[1] But its features tend to change with the change of scene. · The duty of the Goel merges into that of the guardians of the peace. The change from a family to a village community shifts the responsibility on to persons who are fellow-villagers, but not of the same family; hence the *raison d'être* of the *lex talionis* disappears, and its place is taken by the fine of *wergild*. The Hebrews, on the contrary, retain the archaic form. Alongside of the passage in Deut. xxi. defining the responsibility of a village for a murder within its mark, we have the one in Deut. xix. defining the rights of the Goel. And in Num. xxxv. 31, 32, is *The avenging of blood.*

---

[1] *Cf.* § 24, p. 45.

maintained the old law of retaliation; no wergild is allowed. This persistence of the old form is explained by the facts commented on in § 19 as to the fusion of family and village life. Indeed, in Deut. xix. 5, 6, the elements of the fusion are still distinguishable. We have already noted in § 20 the *communal* aspect of the man who "goeth into the wood with his *neighbour* (רעהו) to hew wood;" now, in the same village we see the *"familiar"* position of the same villager and his family towards his neighbour as the "avenger of blood" (גאל הדם). And thus, too, is explained the existence of the *lex talionis* in spite of the tendency to wergild.

The raising
of seed.

The raising of seed to a deceased kinsman is an interesting survival of a still earlier custom. Its foundation is the religious desire for children qualified to offer sacrifices for the repose of the dead, but not necessarily to inherit paternal property—a distinction which, as we have already noted (§ 9), is still maintained in India. Taking this religious desire in connection with the condition of society depicted in § 9, arising out of the reciprocal influence of nomad and pastoral institutions, the Hebrew survivals at once admit of explanation. Probably the obligation arose, as elsewhere, out of the custom of giving a husband assistance during his lifetime. But in any case, compliance with the obligation was not detrimental to the next of kin, seeing that the child had no claim to his father's property. As the family developed into the village and communism became the rule, there would still be no detriment to the next of kin; in fact, the interchange of function between Goel and fellow-villager, which has already been illustrated in the case of blood-revenge, is paralleled in Germany, where assistance in this matter also is a communal duty.[1] But as soon as the village community began to break up into private estates, and descent to children thereby acquired strength, compliance with the obligation became equivalent to cutting one's self off from the succession, a stage which is indicated in Ruth iv. 6. This, and the disintegration of family life which follows upon it, render it impossible to call upon kinsmen of a remote kind to fulfil the duty, and thus arises that special form of the custom known as the *levirate*, where the duty is confined to the brother-in-law of the widow. This is the stage reached in India and in the law of Deut. xxv. 5 *ff.*, which, by limiting the custom to cases where brethren " dwell together," *i.e.*, where the family village is not broken up, shows us the custom in the last stage of decay.[2] Still investigation of this custom, and of that of blood-revenge, has enabled us to see that down to a late period of Hebrew life the next of kin retained an important place in village economy.

§ 27. We have now to consider the position of the The Shofe-
Shôfetîm—the judges whom tradition places between
the village community and the kingship of Saul and
David.

tim.

[1] Grimm, *Rechtsalterthümer*, 445, which is probably as remarkable a law as was ever recorded.

[2] On the " raising of seed " I may refer to my article in the *Theological Review*, October 1878, where the authorities are arranged.

The charac-
ter of feudal
lordships.

In every country there exist, side by side with the free village communities, others whose freedom is limited by the authority exercised over them by a superior lord. In these communities the villagers are not slaves or bondsmen; they possess most of the rights of the free communities, and the power of the lord has definite limits, but still the villagers owe certain services to their lord. Tenure of land in the village is not by right of the community, but by favour of the lord; and in return service in war, or in manual labour, or in produce, is due from the villager.

Their origin.

These lordships arise in three principal ways. In some cases the natural vicissitudes of families tend to throw an accumulation of land into the hands of an individual; in others, and this is perhaps the most frequent form, large tracts are granted by the crown from the common land to some doughty knight, who holds them by military service, and naturally carves out minor holdings to be held in like manner from himself; in yet other cases the various classes within the community develop into two distinct groups, of which one is superior to the other. Of these three ways, we shall find direct examples of the first two in Israel; the third will need a closer examination.

The internal
change of the
village com-
munity.

A. In Ger-
many.

The impulse to the transformation of the German village community came from the officers and servants of the village—artisans, labourers, and the like—together with those mentioned in § 21. All these work for the community, and in return are fed and protected by it. Although, therefore, they i. The rising influence of the artisan classes. have no voice in the government of the village, they form an element which the governing body cannot but take into account. In many respects their interests are one with the interests of the communists, and in that point of view the expression "entire village" or "commune" is used for the whole body of villagers and servants. As these latter grow more numerous and rich, the communists are the more compelled to spare them and give heed to them; "and so," says Von Maurer, "there arose in many village communities a similar struggle to that which took place in the old towns, and the results of it in earlier and later times, and in different communities, have been very varied."[1] The general result was that either the outsiders were received into the community; or, if they did not succeed in that, yet succeeded in ejecting the old communists from their position as the ruling community, and themselves acquired a share in the village government. In this case the old communists were wont to content themselves with the possession of the common mark, and in this respect to become more and more exclusive against the broader commune, reserving to themselves the use and regulation of the common mark [in fact, becoming "lords of the manor"], while the care of other village matters was left to the "entire commune."[2]

In some instances, however, the evolution varied ii. The development of the upper class. in a remarkable way. The old families became *personally exclusive*, in such a way that the full

---

[1] Von Maurer, *Dorfverfassung*, i. 163.   [2] *Ibid.*, i. 165.

burgher right was no longer attainable by possession of house and land, but simply by descent from an old family, and consequently became dependent upon ancestral qualification. This form was assumed in many Swiss communes.

B. In Rome.   If we compare these records with the traditions of early Rome, which we have Sir H. Maine's authority for looking upon as a coalescence of two or more village communities, we see that identical forces are at work here also. In the Patricians we have the "full burgers" of Germany; only the Patricians have preserved a link with the earlier period in their organisation into tribes which has been lost in Germany. In the Clients and Plebeians we recognise the servants of the German communes. Clients and Plebeians, as they become powerful, are at length admitted to a share of government by votes in the *comitia centuriata*, an institution whose relation to the *comitia curiata* is precisely parallel to that of the "whole commune" to the "inner commune" of Germany. In Rome, however, circumstances welded the entire community into one homogeneous body, whereas in Germany the comparative isolation of the towns resulted in the growth of numerous baronies. In Rome, on the contrary, though supreme power was vested in the two Prætors, Judices, or Consuls, these remained the servants of the city. These, it need hardly be said, were elected at the *comitia centuriata*, and represent accordingly the result of the fusion of the full and partially qualified villagers.

Passing to Semitic peoples, we find a similarity between the Roman and Phœnician organisation which has often been remarked. The tribes which appear in the Roman patriciate appear also in the patriciate of Carthage and other Phœnician cities, and the details have long since been worked out by Movers. But in Tyre and its colonies is found an organisation similar to the Roman consulate, viz., the two Sufets, and their position and functions are of great importance. Originally, as Movers has shown, Tyre was simply an island temple, around which a great city gradually grew up. " Since Tyre became a considerable city both parts had separate governments with two chief magistrates. This arrangement must have lasted down to a late period, as may be inferred from the political separation between Island-Tyre and Old-Tyre, several traces of which remain. . . . The inference from these notices, that the double town had two chief magistrates, is more definitely indicated by the mention of the ' princes of Tyre ' in the days when Tyre had as yet no king. Still more decisive is the mention in all Tyrian colonies of *two* Sufets." [1] Then, after pointing out how the same dual government continued under the kings, Movers passes on to note that in Carthage one Sufet was superior to the other, and continues : " These apparently contradictory notices point to a difference of rank. On closer examination of the accounts, it comes out that the second Sufet was appointed to supervise

[1] *Die Phönizier,* ii. (i.) 532 *ff.*

the first, and was chosen from another family, usually from one whose hostility to that of his colleague was a sufficient guarantee for the reliability of his control."[1]

D. In Assyria. A similar institution, with the identical appellation, appears to have existed in Assyria. In the inscriptions of King Sargon there occur several times certain "sapiti," who, in appellation, are evidently one with the שפטים, as the ṭi is written with the symbol indicating ט and not ת. The context of the various passages is: "Judges (sapiṭi) and prefects I set over them (*i.e.*, certain conquered nations)."

"With the satraps of my country, my wise men, my doctors, my nobles, my judges (sapiṭi), . . . I exercised dominion over them."[2]

"Over all those countries I set prefects (sapiṭi) to administer justice."

And in another inscription, "sapiṭi u saknati," judges and satraps are mentioned together; saknatu being a title of Sargon himself.[3] These sapiṭi, therefore, form an additional link between the shôfêt of the Hebrews and the consul of Rome.

Identity of type between Baron, Consul, and Sufet. Evidently identical forces were at work in these four cases, modified, of course, by the special circumstances of each case. In Phœnicia, Germany, and Rome we see the tribe settling in the town or village, and gathering round itself a mixed multitude of servants and outsiders, to whom finally it became neces-

---

[1] *Die Phönizier,* ii. (i.) 536.

[2] Inscription of Sargon, lines 32, 65; in Ménant, *Manuel de la Langue Assyrienne,* pp. 318, 321.

[3] Oppert, *Dour-Sarkayan,* p. 4, l. 23; p. 13, l. 16.

sary to give some share of civic government. And
the result is different in outward seeming only. The
consul of Rome, the sufet of Carthage, is at bottom
one with the sapiṭu of Assyria and the baron of
Germany. In Germany the lack of a central con-
trolling power left the different towns to struggle
against each other, and to become the prey of the
feudal lords. In Rome and Phœnicia, where the
town was the centre of political influence both for
itself and the country round it, the burgers possessed
an influence and power which counterbalanced that
of the consul and sufet. In Assyria, where a military
despotism ruled, we see the sapiṭu exercising the
functions of viceroy or duke, combining the independence of the baron with the subordination of the
consul. That the sapiṭu often set up a rival kingdom of more or less endurance is matter of Assyrian
history; and even in Rome the consul developed in
time into the irresponsible dictator, and the dictator
into the emperor.

§ 28. In Israel we have already points of contact Comparison
with the phenomena we have just investigated. We with Israel.
know that in Israel, as in Carthage, there were tribes
and families; that these developed, as in Germany
and Rome, into village communities; and we have
the shôfetîm, corresponding in name to the sufets of
Phœnicia. The question arises: Are the shôfetîm
of the Hebrews traceable to the same source as consuls and sufets? Are they, in fact, the barons of the
middle age of Hebrew history?

Origin in
personal
prowess.
One source of baronial power—personal ability—
meets us in the Book of Judges. Gideon is the
younger son of a poor family, but his successful
raid against Midian gains for him sovereignty over
Shechem. He hands down the office to his children,
but they are ousted by the cunning of Abimelech.
Similarly, military success secures for Jephthah the
lordship of Gilead. Among heroes of lesser legen-
dary fame, we read of similar attempts to found
dynasties. And yet the power of the judge was not
altogether absolute. The submission of Ephraim and
Gilead to Gideon and Jephthah was voluntary, and
could hardly otherwise have been enforced by the
judges. In this respect Samuel is a typical judge.
At Ramah, where his house was, he seems to have
exercised all lordly functions, judicial and religious,
and to have been recognised as lord by his towns-
men. But when he went "on circuit" as a judge,
his functions did not supersede those of the "elders"
of the towns, as we see from his visit to the elders of
Bethlehem.[1]

Foundations
by national
gift.
Those are the successful attempts at aggrandise-
ment of simple citizens. Lordships of equitable
foundation in the will of the nation are not wanting.
The most notable are the gifts to Joshua of Timnath-
serah, "the city which he asked," and to Caleb of
the city of Hebron. This latter instance, which has
already afforded matter for consideration, it is necessary to quote again. "They gave them (the Levites)
the city of Arba, the father of Anak, which is Hebron,

---

[1] *Cf.* 1 Sam. ix. with chap. xvi., *passim.*

in the hill of Judah, with the suburbs (מגרשה) round about it. But the *fields* (שדה) of the city and the *villages* (חצריה) thereof gave they to Caleb, the son of Jephunneh." The "migrash" we have already seen to be parallel to the "arable mark," and the "sâdeh" to the "pasture mark" of the Teutonic communities. In the inhabitants of the חצרים we have the "hewers of wood and drawers of water," the servants of the Teutonic communities. And thus there appear here the same two classes that we meet in all feudal communities, only that in this instance, more than in most, the arrangement parallels that of an ordinary feudal manor of the Middle Ages. In both Teuton and Hebrew the villagers suffer only a nominal curtailment of their freedom within the precincts of the village; while over the common land and the extra-communal settlers the lord's power tends continually to increase.

Thus far the Hebrew lords are parallel rather to the barons of Germany than to the consuls of Rome or the sufets of Phœnicia. And yet the deputation of the elders of Gilead to Jephthah seems to indicate that in Israel, as in Rome and Tyre, single towns or villages outgrew the communal form of government, and elected rulers, who in some cases may have developed into barons, in others, under the combined influence of the religion and the monarchy, have never exceeded the limits of magisterial jurisdiction. To such cases I take the law to refer: "Judges (שפטים) and officers shalt thou make thee in all thy gates" (Deut. xvi, 18). In accordance with this

Development from decadent village communities

is the manner in which the shôfetîm are mentioned
in Deuteronomy.   The baron who disfranchises
his poorer neighbour acts entirely within his own
jurisdiction (chap. xv. *passim*), or at least subject
only to the judgment of God (אלהים, Exod. xxi. 6).
In the rest of the book the shôfêt appears quite independent (except in chap. xxi.) of the elders, and it is
remarkable that, unlike them, his name is quite
unconnected with any traditional " dooms."   On the
contrary, he is the declarer of judgment in cases to
which the traditional law would not apply.   All this
indicates that he is a newer formation than the elders,
the result of a newer order of things.   And in this
too he resembles the mediæval baron.   For this latter
also is bound by the traditions and customs of his
manor; only in cases of doubtful application or of
new growth does his court come into operation.

Altogether, therefore, we look upon the shôfêt as
the result of the development or partial decadence
of the village community.   Called into existence by
the needs of his time, and rising for a brief period,
or in individual cases, into a dignity of power and
wealth, he is in turn overtaken by the wave of progress and sinks to the position of an officer, powerful,
but yet a servant.

V. Survivals.

§ 29. WE now pass to the survivals or modified
features of communal life to be found in Israel.
Here it is necessary to bring into prominence a
principle which has been implicitly assumed in the
preceding paragraphs, viz., the contemporaneous
existence of divergent types and features. It is not
unusual, in dealing with the Pentateuch, to set off
or cancel one law against another; to assume that
of two contradictory enactments one must be earlier
or later than the other. However justifiable this
may be philologically, it is unjustifiable and untrue
sociologically. In all countries which have passed
through several stages of social life, institutions of
all periods exist side by side. In our own highly
developed land there exist, alongside of great cities
wholly absorbed in commerce, little communities
which have, as it were yesterday, just given up the
" shifting severalty." Even in the great cities themselves, tenure by freehold and registered title co-
exists with tenure by court rolls and tenpenny-nails.
There is no reason to suppose that it was otherwise .
in Israel. The Song of Deborah touches lightly on
the pasture lands of Reuben and the ships and
havens of Dan and Asher. We cannot suppose that

the whole country progressed at the same rate. Rather we must conclude the contrary, and in dealing with survivals be prepared to find not only that institutions of different periods coexist, but that they influence each other; here, that a feudal lord is restrained by the commune; there, that the tribe of Levi has retained some old forgotten custom.

Periodical redistribution of lands. § 30. One of the most striking features of the village community is the periodical redistribution of the village lands (§ 17). " There appears to be no country inhabited by an Aryan race in which traces do not remain of the ancient periodical redistribution. It has continued to our own day in the Russian villages.[1] Among the Hindu villagers there are widely extending traditions of the practice, and it was doubtless the source of certain usages . . . which have survived to our day in England and Germany."[2] Nor is the custom confined to Aryan peoples. Among the Afghans a custom of redistribution exists, or existed until lately, and is very apposite. Like the Hebrews, the Afghans are divided into tribes and gentes. The tribes have each their separate territory, but within the tribe the allotment of the several gentes is determined by lot every seven years, and consequently the lots of individual families change at the expiration of each septennium.[3] This custom survives in Israel

[1] Details in Maine's *Anc. Law*, 267.

[2] Maine, *Vill. Comm.*, 82; *cf.* Von Maurer, *Dorfverfassung*, i. 35.

[3] *Cf.* Kemble, *Saxons in England*, i. 39.

in the year of release and the year of jubilee. The laws relative to these it is necessary to place clearly before our mind's eye, treating them at the outset, in pursuance of the principle just indicated, as practically intercontemporaneous.

In Deut. xv. 1–11 is an enactment that once in every seven years all debts due from a brother Israelite shall be released. Laws relating to redistribution.

In verses 12–18 is a law that a Hebrew slave, after serving six years, shall be set free in the seventh, being furnished liberally, upon his departure, from his master's flock, and floor, and winepress. But if the slave be satisfied with his servitude, he may be formally bound down in perpetuity.

In Exod. xxi. 2–6 is an identical law with respect to the release of the slave after six years' service, with this important difference, that *he is to go out precisely as he came in.* But he, too, if he prefer servitude, may be made a slave for ever.

In Exod. xxiii. 10, 11, follows a law that every seventh year the land shall " rest and lie still."

In Lev. xxv. 2–7 is a law identical with that in Exod. xxiii., followed by another containing the essence of the Exodic and Deuteronomic laws respecting slaves, but with a radical alteration. According to Leviticus, the release of debts and slaves is only a portion of a general readjustment of social existence which is to take place, not at variable periods, but at the recurrence of every seventh Sabbath year—roundly, in every fifty years.

E

Fall into two groups. These laws at once fall into two groups, one with a period of seven years, the other with a period of fifty years. We will take the seven years' group first.

A. The seven years' group: its two sections. § 31. The seven years' group again divides into two sections: one in which the seven years is an invariable limit, fixed by some independent *terminus a quo;* the second in which the seven years is a variable limit, changing with the necessities of each individual case.

The section of fixed terminus. The first section contains the law of release (Deut. xv. 1–11), with the law of the seventh year fallow (Exod. xxiii. 10, 11; Lev. xxv. 2–7). This latter law shows us at once that we are dealing with the regulations of a typical village community. It is of fundamental importance to the proper enjoyment of **Applicable to pure village communities.** the land by the villagers that no portion should be unduly or irregularly worked by one family to the detriment of others. Thus, in Germany, " the mode of enjoying the fields remained a communal matter, to be arranged not by individuals, but rather by the entire community. Among such matters are the sequence of crops, . . . *the alternation of ploughing and fallow years,*" &c.[1] The division of the cultivated land into three great fields had in view the same object, that each field should be fallow once in three years.[2]

The same holds good of the law of release. Debtor and creditor are on a footing of absolute equality.

---

[1] Von Maurer, *Dorfverfassung,* i. 36.   [2] Maine, *Vill. Comm.,* 79, 80.

They are "neighbours" (רֵעַ) and "brethren." There
is no mention of servitude such as there is in the
verses of the following law. Rather they are on that
footing of equality which forbids the creditor to
enter the debtor's house to fetch a pledge.[1] With
the seventh year all obligation and all claim is
summarily cut short.

If these laws do not absolutely imply the periodical redistribution of the land—the shifting severalty,
as it is technically termed—they are well explained
by that hypothesis. If once in every seven years
the land is redistributed, then the debtor starts again
on an equality with his neighbours; the accidents
that temporarily reduced him to poverty are removed.
Question of servitude in such case cannot possibly
arise. The loan becomes a matter of communal
help, like the customs discussed in § 24. Whether
or not the fallow year was the year of release is not
explicitly stated. One would imagine that it was.
It would probably be more satisfactory to the
villagers to enter upon land comparatively fresh
rather than on land already worked out by a neighbour. Difficulty of existence there would be none.
To have the whole tract fallow during one year of a
series comes to the same thing in the end as having
a fraction fallow during each year of the series. If
the German villages took in enough land to be able
always to have one-third lying fallow, the Hebrews
may surely be credited with "kind wit" enough to
do the like in their own way. How they came to

*Explicable
on assump-
tion of shift-
ing severalty.*

---

[1] Deut. xxiv. 10 *ff.*

take every seventh year is perhaps explicable by
reference to the Sabbath. This we know now to be
an old Semite festival. We have seen the influence
of religion on the Hebrew village, and that the priest
is one of its officers. With these influences at hand,
the redistribution of land would naturally partake of
a religious character and fall into a septennium.

B. The sec-
tion of vari-
able ter-
minus.

We now come to the second section, in which the
septennium has a variable ending. This section contains the laws in Exod. xxi. 2–6 and Deut. xv. 12–18
concerning the release and possible disfranchisement
of a slave. Here the relations of debtor and creditor
are very different to those in the first section. In

Applicable
to manorial
villages.

the אדון or lord, rich in flocks, herds, and vineyards,
and indulging in polygamy, we see evidently the
baron of § 28. And this implies a corresponding
change in the debtor. He is not the freeman of the
pure village community, but the freeman of the
manorial village. In such a village there is obviously no " shifting severalty." Tenure is by will of
the lord. When, for whatever reason, the borrower
becomes the slave of the lord, he yields up his possession in the village; and when he is released from
bondage, the lord, if so minded, may grant him
another share. This subordination of the tenant is
marked in the Exodic law. All that the slave
acquires during his servitude is the lord's. Even
wife and children, if he have married during his
servitude, belong to the lord: freedom of birth following here the female line, in the archaic fashion.
All that the Hebrew retains in the manorial village

is his personal freedom, the right to be placed personally on an equality with his brethren of the free
villages. In the Deuteronomic law occurs the additional command to "furnish" the departing slave
liberally. This I take to mean that there had grown
up among the Hebrews a practice similar to that
known in Europe as "commendation," whereby a
poor tribesman accepts a gift of cattle from the chief,
and so becomes the vassal of his chief.[1] The Hebrew
custom is not exactly parallel to the European commendation, but the resemblance is sufficiently close
to permit one to suggest that the "furnishing" of
the Hebrew tenant is the relic of a transaction by
which, in return for service and homage, the tenant
was "set up" in the village with land and cattle.

These two sections of the "seven years' group" of
laws are, therefore, to be looked upon as belonging to
two distinct aspects of agricultural life, no doubt of
contemporaneous existence with each other. The
section of absolute septennium deals with pure village
communities, and is based upon the periodical redistribution of village land: the period of relative septennium deals with manorial villages, and is modified
in accordance with their peculiar characteristics.
The two sections preserve, therefore, in their matter
—not in their form—a relic of the most archaic
period of agricultural life. Almost inexplicable if
they be supposed to have originated at a late period
of Hebrew history, they present no difficulty if we
assume them to be the survival of a period through

[1] Maine, *Early Hist. of Inst.*, 157 ff.

which every agricultural community has at the outset passed.

Decay of the redistribution. § 32. Hebrew history shows that in Israel, as elsewhere, this communal redistribution tended to decay.
The influence of commerce and of the large towns
no doubt aided the internal disruption of the commune. The periodical redistribution first became
obsolete, and the year of fallow followed it. The
growth of personal ownership, and the haste to become
rich which marked the Solomonic period, could not
abide the simple mode of life with which alone the fallow was compatible. "What shall we eat the seventh
year? Behold we shall not sow, nor gather our increase," said the farmers. And so the fallow departed,
mourned by the priests, who looked back with regret
to the old times when the land "kept her Sabbaths."[1]

Oppression of the manorial lords. As the commune decayed baronial oppression increased. The dealing of Ahab with Naboth's vine-
yard was but one instance out of many. "Woe
unto them that join house to house, that lay field to
field, till there be no place."[2] "Among my people
are found wicked men: they lay wait, as he that
setteth snares: they set a trap, they catch men. As
a cage is full of birds, so are their houses full of
deceit; therefore they are become great and waxen
rich. They are waxen fat, they shine; yea, they
overpass the deeds of the wicked: they judge not the
cause, the cause of the fatherless: and the right of
the needy they do not judge."[3]

[1] *Cf.* Maine, *Vill. Comm.*, 87, for the decay of the redistribution.
[2] Isaiah v. 8.
[3] Jeremiah v. 25-28.

That this state of things would produce an outcry Desire for revival of re-distribution. from many for the restitution of the old order is easily imaginable, and popular leaders would not be wanting. But how remedy the evil? How restore to the communities their old rights and privileges without unduly trenching upon rights and posses-sions that had since been acquired? The year of jubilee is the Hebrew solution of the problem.

The principle of the year of jubilee is a compro- Satisfied by the year of jubilee. mise which, curiously enough, has been put into practice elsewhere. The borough of Newtown upon Ayr, in Scotland, possessed, as heirs of the old com- Jubilee appears else-where. mune, certain common lands, which, according to ancient custom, were reapportioned among the mem-bers of the corporation every eleven years, and after A.D. 1666 every seven years. This period at length, in the year 1771, was found by the corporation to be too short to allow the holders to make any good use of the lands. Turn the land into private property they could not; but they hit upon the ingenious expedient of distributing the land once only in eight periods, *i.e.*, once in every fifty-seven years. In this way the reversionary right of the commune was preserved intact, while the burger acquired practically a lease of his lot for fifty-seven years. Eventually this period was lengthened to 999 years.[1] Upon this basis the jubilee was arranged. It assumed the con-tinued existence of the village communities sketched in §§ 16, 19, and 20. The fallow in every seventh

---

[1] *New Statistical Account of Scotland*, v. 91. For this remarkable instance I am indebted to Mr. G. L. Gomme, F.S.A.

year is of course also retained (Lev. xxv. 17). Had
none but pure village communities been in question,
the law in Deut. xv. 1–11 might still have sufficed.
But there were the manorial villages with their own
code of rules; there were the towns, with their necessarily varied requirements. The seven years' redistribution would scarcely benefit the free villager, and
would be absolutely unfair to the lords of manors.
So the redistribution was deferred until the seventh
fallow year. Thereby the villager was converted
into a lessee for forty-nine years, on which security
he could borrow a sufficient sum. The same rule
was applied to personal service; and thus the manorial
lords were converted practically into tenants for life
of their manors, their children sinking at the jubilee
Its practical result. into ordinary villagers. In this way the extinction
of the ruling class was prepared surely and equit-
ably. The villager also had all the advantages of
both systems, for his tenure had precisely the same
value as a modern lease (Lev. xxv. 27, 50–52); and
if the value decreased as the lease neared its end,
there was the compensation that assistance also was
only needed for a short period.

Its rigidity and remedy. Equitable as was this law, it was too rigid for
general use, and the prospect of a simultaneous
termination of baronial tenures cannot, from what
we know of the "princes of Israel," have been a
pleasant one. A means of amelioration was found
in the "Goel," whose functions have lately been
discussed. To him it was permitted to foreclose, so
to speak, the mortgage raised by a kinsman, upon

paying the proportionate value of the unexpired lease. From this two results might be expected. The solidarity of communal life was kept up. For since the Goel exercised the functions of both kinsman and fellow-villager, it was manifestly to his interest to keep kin and village free from baronial interference. At the same time, the lords, instead of finding themselves at the jubilee without any estate, would gradually be extinguished by receiving from time to time the value of their leases in a manner which recalls the aim and operation of our own Copyhold Acts. And in this way, the devisers of the jubilee succeeded in doing fairly practical justice to the great lords, while at the same time restoring the primitive village.

But they were not able to carry out their scheme in its entirety. They had to make exceptions which show that social life had irrevocably passed beyond the communal stage. The right of redemption in the large towns had to be limited to twelve months after the sale. Obviously, commerce could not be carried on if some such restriction had not been adopted. In the smaller towns, however, which were presumably devoted chiefly to agricultural requirements, the right of redemption continued up to the jubilee. But in the case of the Levites, the exceptions show how tenaciously that tribe adhered to its old privileges, and indicate that the jubilee is not so much an innovation as a revival of the old. Even in great towns, "if a Levite be the Goel [I follow the received text, which presents to me no

Necessity for compromise.

Conservatism of the devisers of the law.

difficulty] the house that was sold, and the city of his possession shall go out [*i.e.,* return to the Levite] in the jubilee" (ver. 33). And not only was this restriction removed, but the "mark" of their smaller towns retains all the old communal privilege : it may not be sold at all : " it is their perpetual possession " (ver. 34). Forced to admit a compromise for the laity, the Levite stoutly maintained his own ancient rights.

Such, then, is the year of jubilee, the last effort to reconcile the old with the new, the simpler with the more complex mode of life ; a relic of the old age of the commune, while the Sabbath year is a relic of its youth.

§ 33. Another feature of communal life is the right of sanctuary. In later times it appears as a prerogative of religion or the Church, but in its origin it is an attribute of the village community. Sanctuary did not originally imply that immunity from punishment that it came to mean in the Middle Ages. In its essence it is only temporary, the safeguarding of a refugee until his crime has been sufficiently proved to justify the commune in giving him up. Even the Hebrew law did not extend to wilful criminals.

Right of sanctuary.

Under this aspect of temporary security sanctuary is a necessary corollary from the constitution of a village community. Every village is fenced in from without, and assumes a collective responsibility for the deeds of its villagers. Concurrently the village

Necessary to the constitution of a village community.

naturally claims a right to adjudicate upon its own
quarrels, and an immunity from the jurisdiction of
foreign judges. And this immunity is a jealously
guarded right of the village. Hence it follows
immediately that if a man takes refuge in the
village, his pursuers will not be allowed to seize him
by force, as they would within their own bounds,
but must proceed in an orderly way to adduce
evidence of the justice of their pursuit. If they do
so, then the criminal is delivered up, but meanwhile
his liberty is respected; and this is the original right
of sanctuary. In some cases sanctuary only existed
for a certain number of days, or until the regular
court of justice could assemble. It is in this way
that Von Maurer traces sanctuary from the right of
immunity in Germany.[1] In England, it is shown in
a paper in an early volume of " Archæologia,"[2] that
sanctuary was originally in the gift of the king, and
belonged not exclusively to the church of a town,
but to the town alone. In the Rig - Veda, among
the early Aryans, Professor Ludwig has found sanctuary under the name " vidatha," which, while prin-
cipally used for a religious assembly, is by derivation
and original use the term for a community of relatives,
either by blood or tribe. And its communal character appears in the old custom of presenting one's
bride to the " vidatha."[3] How sanctuary came to Its connection with
be a religious institution is easily explained. In religion.
course of time the right was abused, and became a

---

[1] Von Maurer, *Dorfverfassung*, ii. 162–171.
[2] Vol. viii. pp. 1–44.   [3] Ludwig, *Rig-Veda*, iii. 259, 261.

public nuisance, which eventually had, as in England, to be put down by the strong hand of authority, and only the Church and a few great corporations were strong enough to maintain their old privilege.

Sanctuary in Israel.

Of the general communal sanctuary in Israel there is a trace in Deut. xxiii. 15, 16, which enacts that any town or village shall be an asylum for an escaped slave. In Exod. xxi. 14, the altar, presumably any one of the numerous village altars, is mentioned as a refuge. In the cities of refuge the sanctuary is used only for the mitigation of the revenge of blood, a point in which, as we have already seen (§ 26), Israel retained the archaic *lex talionis.* Assuming the right of sanctuary to be inherent in each village

The cities of refuge.

community, one would take the cities of refuge to be a relic of this privilege. With this the facts seem to be in accordance. It is the town itself, and not any holy place in it, that constitutes the sanctuary. Within the " border" of the town the slayer is safe; without it he is liable to death.[1] Nor is it the priest, but the " elders " of the town—the communal authorities—who are to judge of his fitness to remain or to be delivered up.[2] So, too, the elders of the " Goel's " town are to act on his behalf;[3] so that the procedure is throughout one of entirely communal character. The sanctuary, too, is one of the limited character noted above as the original feature of the privilege. According to Deuteronomy, the decision rests with the elders of the town of refuge (chap. xix. 12); according to Numbers and Joshua, the

[1] Num. xxxv. 26, 27. [2] Josh. xx. 4. [3] Deut. xix. 12.

decision rests with the "congregation." What this means we see from the passages in Joshua and Samuel which show that the people met (either in body or by their elders) in Mizpeh or some other place to transact business of national justice.[1] The divergence is interesting. On the one hand, Deuteronomy clearly preserves the more archaic form, in which the decision of sanctuary rests with the elders of the town. On the other hand, Numbers and Joshua, by introducing the "congregation" as the supreme authority, remind us that in Israel, as elsewhere, the sanctuary of promiscuous towns was no doubt abused, and that the nation as a body had to regulate the privilege. And as we know that the democratic congregation only existed during what I have called the baronial—the pre-monarchical period—perhaps we may infer that the establishment of definite towns of sanctuary appertains to that period. That such towns should be priestly settlements was natural; for already, in treating of the jubilee, we have seen how the Levites maintained their old rights, and, as framers and utterers of the law, they had every opportunity in this instance of preserving their power.

§ 34. We have now reviewed the growth and decay of communal life in Israel. We may fitly close this section on survivals by examining an ideal survival to be found in the Book of Ezekiel. That

An ideal survival.

---

[1] *e.g.*, Gilgal, Josh. xiv. 6; Shiloh, Josh. xxi. 2; Mizpeh, 1 Sam. vii. 5, 6; Ramah, 1 Sam. viii. 3.

prophet, in the 48th chapter of his book, lays down
the boundaries of the ideal land of Israel in the
manner shown on the accompanying diagram.   It is
interesting to observe how closely he follows the
arrangement of an ideal village community as it was
sketched in § 17.   The straight strips of land allotted
to the tribes correspond to the fields allotted to the
members of a commune, and are grouped as sym-
metrically as possible around a centre space.   On
each side of the centre space is one marked for the
" prince."   Out of it he may grant portions to his
children, who shall possess such shares in perpetuity,
being, in fact, new members of the commune.   Out
of it also he may grant portions to his courtiers, but
these, having presumably an inheritance elsewhere,
must surrender their share in the " prince's portion "
in the jubilee.   In fact, the " prince's portion " is
the waste, the unoccupied land of the commune.
The square space within the waste is divided into
three strips of pasture land, for the priests, the
Levites, and the city.   This latter is again divided
in a remarkable manner.   In the exact centre stands
the town (marked A); around it is a space of 250
reeds, or 1500 cubits in breadth (marked B), which
is stated to be for suburbs, or " migrash," which we
identified by means of the 2000 cubits' breadth of
the Levitical cities as the arable mark of Teutonic
communities.   Beyond this, again, the residue (C, C),
is to be for food to them that serve the city.   This
is clearly none other than the pasture mark; and if
these servants of the city are not free burgers, we

Dan.
Asher.
Naphtali.
Manasseh.
Ephraim.
Reuben.
Judah.

Prince.	Priests.	Prince.
	D ⌐E	
	Levites.	
	C B A C	

Benjamin.
Simeon.
Issachar.
Zebulun.
Gad.

have another instance of those unfree dwellers on the common whom we noticed in § 28. Here, therefore, we have repeated the whole of the organisation of the village community. And not by accident, for in treating of the sanctuary the prophet adopts exactly the same plan, placing the Holy House (D) in the centre of the priests' allotment, and round it the narrow migrash (E) of fifty cubits.[1] Evidently Ezekiel aimed at idealising an arrangement which, either from sight or record, was familiar to him—and to us.

[1] Ezekiel xlv. 1 *ff.*

VI.—The Customs and the Traditions.

§ 35. WHEN writing is unknown, how are customs The preservation of unwritten records of customs; and usages preserved from falling into desuetude? How are the decisions of the elders in doubtful cases handed down for the benefit of posterity? In a two-fold way: first, by symbolical actions—token-deeds, as Ewald happily termed them—of which instances like beating the bounds and tenure by the rod remain to this day; and, secondly, by traditions, symbolical stories—token-tales, if one may say so, which are handed down in the general folk-lore of a people. Such stories, semi-legal precedents, are not unfamiliar: the tradition of Zelophchad's daughters is one such, embodying the prehistoric notion of the duty of heiresses. In this way various dubious points of primitive morality and politics were governed; and the stories which enshrine them stand to primitive Especially moral and political. life in much the same relation as do collections of precedents to modern lawyers and dictionaries of cases of conscience to father confessors.

Many of the stories of the Old Testament appear to me to share this feature of primitive morals, and some of the more obscure I propose here to attempt to elucidate.

The peculiar feature of Abraham's marriage, viz.,

F

Abraham's relation to his wife.

that his wife was 'the daughter of his father, but not the daughter of his mother,' has already been alluded to in § 6, where it formed one of a number of cumulative instances tending to show that paternal kinship was not valued so highly by the early Hebrews as maternal kinship. I deal with it again here, because its reduplication in the life of Isaac forces it upon our attention as a story which possessed some peculiar interest for the Hebrews. And if the hypothesis of the higher estimation of maternal kinship be true, the story really depicts a national custom as contrasted with the divergent customs of surrounding nations. Viewed through modern ideas, the story seems to be merely one of the personal keenness of Abraham and Isaac in taking advantage of a casual incident of relationship between themselves and their wives. But viewed through archaic notions, the story turns upon a national characteristic; and inasmuch as marriages of the Abrahamic kind are common enough under the archaic system, the seeming paradox had no doubt been experienced by many Hebrews, and was certainly well known to all. The incident is a popular enunciation of the doctrine that the suppression of the truth is distinct from the utterance of falsehood.

Absalom and Tamar.

In the story of Absalom and Tamar[1] the same archaic custom forms the foundation. Absalom, enamoured of Tamar, who is his sister on the paternal side, endeavours to gratify his desire by violence; and Tamar, in her ineffectual expostulation, uses

[1] 2 Sam. xiii.

these remarkable words: "Now therefore, I pray thee, speak unto the king; for he will not withhold me from thee.'[1] Such a marriage, though contra-dictory to the Levitical law, would be perfectly admissible under archaic rules.

The story of Judah and Tamar[2] is more complex. Briefly sketched it is this. Tamar had been married to Judah's eldest son, Er, who had died without issue. Onan, the next son, married the widow, but evaded his duty as Goel of raising seed to his brother. He therefore died by the judgment of Yahweh. Then Judah deferred the marriage of the widow with his youngest son, Shelah. Time passed, and Shelah was not given in marriage to Tamar. So Tamar put her widow's garments from her, covered her face with a veil, and sat in an open place, so that Judah thought her to be an harlot, and turned unto her by the way, leaving with her pledges of his love, his signet and bracelet and staff. In course of time it was reported to Judah that Tamar, his daughter-in-law, had played the harlot, and he said: "Let her be burnt." But Tamar brought forth the pledges which Judah had left with her; and Judah said: "She hath been more righteous than I, because I gave her not to Shelah my son."

In this story there appears not only the custom of descent in the female line, but that custom of levirate which was touched on in § 26, and also the joint family life illustrated in § 16. The basis of the levirate has already been explained to be a religious

Judah and Tamar.

---

[1] 2 Sam. xiii. 13.   [2] Gen. xxxviii.

feeling; and therefore the neglect of Judah to marry Tamar to the next of kin to the deceased Er was really the neglect of a religious duty. But in the joint family life Judah was the head of the house; and accordingly, by reason of the extended devolution of the duties of the Goel which was then current, the duty which Judah had neglected to have performed by the intervening kinsman devolved upon himself. Tamar, therefore, was legally in the right, according to the feeling of those times, in looking to Judah as the one by whom, either *per alium* or *per se*, her right should be recognised. Nor was there, under the archaic rule, any bar to her union with Judah, seeing there was no maternal kinship between them. But Judah, as we know, neglected the obligation; the fulfilment was procured only by stratagem, and Tamar was accused of incontinence before her kinsman. But her answer was complete. A sacred obligation had fallen upon the head of the house, and since he showed no disposition to comply with it, Tamar had exerted herself to fulfil the duty.

Tamar worthy of admiration.

From this point of view Tamar's action was honourable; nor can one withhold one's admiration from the wit of the lady who so ingeniously diverted the weaknesses of her kinsman to the attainment of an end which, in those days, was in the eyes of all men emphatically righteous.

Lot's daughters.

If the reader has followed this exposition, he will be prepared to apply the same principles to the explanation of the story of Lot's daughters, who

raised seed by their father to himself.[1] The key to
the story lies in the archaic answer to this question
of primitive casuistry :—

Under the rule that marriage is permissible between those who are related paternally but not
maternally, is a daughter the same relation to her
father that a son is to his mother ? Obviously not. The funda-
A son is related maternally to his mother, and, there- of the story.
fore, may not marry her; a daughter is not related
maternally to her father, and may, therefore, marry
him. Astounding as this distinction may appear, it
is not unworthy of consideration. The fundamental
principle is perhaps not altogether in accordance
with modern taste; but assuming it to exist, it
is clear that under it actions may be classified as
right and wrong just as easily as under any other
principle. Of course the classification will differ
from others made upon different principles, but for
people who accept the principle the classification is
inevitable. Thus where a tribe holds that name and
goods follow from mother to daughter, instead of
from father to son, a man's family name is perpetu-
ated, not by his own children, but by the children of
his mother's daughter—to wit, his sister; while his
own children perpetuate the name of their mother.
And so his affection is attracted, not to his own
children, who perpetuate his wife's mother's name, but
to his sister's children, who perpetuate his own name.
To place his affections upon his own offspring is
wrong, and that it is so is the logical result of this

[1] Gen. xix. 30–38.

principle. That we think otherwise is simply because our feeling as respects the principle differs from his. Similarly for the due understanding of the Lot story, the question is, not what we, or even the later Jews, think of the story; but whether, under the archaic system, any other answer can be given to my question than the one I have given above? If not—if my answer, that a woman may marry her father, is the one and only logical inference from the principle—then an early Hebrew story based upon that inference is moral, notwithstanding modern feeling to the contrary.

The solution of it.

Thus viewed, Lot's story is little more than a variant of the Judah-Tamar story. The same religious desire appears for the preservation of the family name; and the same question arises, whether, in default of the usual kinsman or husband, the woman may take an unwonted spouse? And in each case the answer is the same: Yes; it is strange and unusual, *but it is not wrong.*

Objections.

i. The 'vilificatory' view.

Two objections will no doubt arise in the reader's mind. First, that the Jews themselves—at any rate in later days—regarded these stories differently, and abused one of them to the vilification of their neighbours. Doubtless; but that does not militate against the original purity of the stories. As customs changed, moral feeling, and, with moral feeling, moral anecdotes changed. Such a transmutation of myths is by no means uncommon.

ii. The solution by comparative mythology.

Second, that comparative mythology, by explaining these stories as perversions of the expressions of

natural phenomena, renders them, in the first instance, innocuous. But the school of comparative
mythology has never been able to explain how these
perverted expressions ever gained currency in their
human dress, supposing them to have had a wicked
bias from the beginning. If the generations during
which the change from physical to human phenomena
took place were as greatly shocked as succeeding
ages by the tone of the stories, why did they con-
tinue to repeat them? Either they perceived the
base tone and did not object to it, or else they did
not perceive it. The first alternative will hardly be
accepted; the second is in accordance with my
doctrine, and is explained by it. No evil tendency
was perceived, because, in fact, there was none to
perceive.

Whether or not, therefore, Judah and Tamar, Lot *The stories are questions of casuistry.* and his daughters, were solar personages, the fact
remains that the facts of the stories as narrated are
explicable in a way which not only removes from
them the stigma which they have derived from being
viewed with modern eyes, but even gives them a
distinctly moral character, rendering them, in fact,
as I have endeavoured to show, interesting examples
of the casuistic questions which perplexed the earliest
Hebrew doctors of the law.

§ 36. The view here taken of the influence of *The origin of law.* popular custom and feeling upon folk-tales is applicable in a great degree to the legal records of the
customs. The various laws which have been passed

under review bear a judicial rather than a legislative
aspect.   In each case the enactment has been traced,
not to a reform or an innovation, but to some old
popular usage which needed regulation.   Even the
year of jubilee, which has an exceptionally legislative
aspect, is intended, not to introduce new tenures, but
to uphold and revivify the old.   Instead of marking
out new lines of progress, the Hebrew laws are
simply explanatory and regulative of lines already
existing.

At the same time there are, in the existing form
of the records, undeniable attempts at giving a
purely legislative turn to the judicial laws.   It
seems well, therefore, to indicate briefly the relation
in which these two aspects, the earlier and the later,
stand to each other.

In § 4 it was observed that there was little differentiation of function in early society.   The same
individual fulfils the function of father, chief, and
priest.   Whenever, therefore, disputes arise in the
tribe upon any point of communal life, it comes
before the chief for decision.   From that decision
there is, of course, no appeal, except the radical one
of departure from the tribe.   In this way a rude
kind of law arises, namely, obedience to the will of
the chief.[1]   It is law, however, of a peculiar kind.
It is fragmentary and shifting.   It accumulates in
no orderly way, but simply as one dispute after
another brings with it a necessity for a decision upon
the disputed point.   It is not by any means neces-

The head of the tribe is the primitive judge ;

[1] Maine, *Ancient Law*, 4, 5.

sarily self-consistent, for there is no check upon the
caprice of the chief. And even with the best inten-
tions on the part of chief and people, the lack of
writing materials and other accessories of docu-
mentary preservation would render it next to impossible to hand down the various traditions clearly and
coherently. Such law as this, in which the chief is
the sole fountain of justice, is a common feature in
all books of travel;[1] familiar instances of a similar
state of things meet us in the judgment of Solomon
and the numerous Oriental stories of the ready wit
of the Kadhi.

But these fragmentary decisions, though they give
us one side of early law, and show us the origin of
the later legislator, do not form the great foundation
of law. From their very nature they have no co-
herence of their own, and have no guiding principle
which would enable them to form the basis of a
future code. For that basis we must look elsewhere.
If we contemplate the life of a tribe, it at once
becomes clear that its existence depends upon a
general observance of certain broad laws of communal intercourse. Such laws need not necessarily
be formulated. Indeed, we find them observed to a
considerable extent by the lower animals. These
adopt instinctively habits which conduce to their
existence under the peculiar circumstances of their
life. Individuals among human beings show a similar adaptability to their surroundings. In the same

*But his deci-
sions do not
contain the
whole law,
which exists
in the cus-
toms of the
people.*

---

[1] An instance now before me is Speke's *Journal of the Discovery of
the Source of the Nile*, 358, 374.

way do human beings in a society fall instinctively into habits conducive to the welfare of the society.[1] The village community itself is a remarkable example of this. Even if one were inclined to consider that within the circle of Aryan tradition the village community is the work of some ancestors of high intellectual power, it is impossible to investigate the various forms under which it appears in a large continent of varied peoples, like Africa, without seeing that the village community is a social type, to which all tribes, on becoming agricultural, tend unconsciously to conform. These unconsciously adopted habits grow firmer with each generation, the process of evolution tending to increase their stability, as by their means the tribe or people becomes better adapted to its surroundings. These established social habits are the "customs" of a people. Many of them have never been questioned before the chief, but they exist, and they form the basis by which alone the chief's decisions can be interpreted.

The reciprocal influence of decisions and customs. We have now the two factors of ancient law. In the chief and his decisions we have the judicial authority, and in the unwritten traditional body of custom we have the principles upon which the chief acts. And these two interact upon each other. The authority of the chief is reflected, of course, upon the unwritten tradition, and invests the "custom" of the tribe with his own authority. On the other hand,

[1] Maine, *Ancient Law*, 18, 19; and for the general principle, Spencer, *Principles of Sociology*, i. chap. I.

the "custom" has an authority of its own. We know how disinclined all lower races are to forsake the ways of their fathers; how, in some instances, they reject what they clearly see to be improvements. We know how, in our own Middle Ages, it was customary for a son to follow his father's trade. And though this sequacity may be indirectly due in some measure to. chiefly authority, it is undoubtedly attributable to the tendency of all men to remain in a groove which experience has shown to work and to which they are accustomed.[1]

The result of this interaction is that both the "custom" and the "decisions" acquire equal authority; and when at length writing comes into use and the "decisions" are embodied in a rude code, there rises up a "law" consisting of both the written "decisions" and the unwritten "custom." This is a point of some importance, for a "custom" is usually thought to be less binding than a "law" or "decision." But the "customs" of English manors are enough to prove the contrary; and I have met with an instance in Indian law in which the written law recognises the unwritten custom as of equal validity with itself. Âsvalâyana's "House-rules" opens the section on marriage with these words :—

The binding force of custom.

" 1. Now there are manifold customs of lands and districts; these must be observed in marriage.

" 2. But that which is general we will now utter."

And the Hindu commentator feels it necessary to note that in case of a conflict between these manifold

---

[1] *Cf.* Maine, *Village Communities*, 67, 68.

customs and the "house-rules," the procedure laid down in the latter is to be followed.[1] Evidently the binding force of a custom is here recognised.

An early code, therefore, possesses peculiar features. To the end it remains of a purely judicial character ; it never inaugurates, but simply registers customs. Fragmentary also it remains, and necessarily so from the circumstances of its growth.   And yet these same circumstances contribute to give the code an underlying unity arising from its direct foundation in social life.   Hence, by going back to such records or information as can be obtained of the type of periods in question, we obtain the unwritten principle on which the code is based.

Application to Hebrew law.

§ 37. Applying these general principles to Hebrew law, we may reconstruct to some extent the unwritten history of the Pentateuchal enactments.   We can at once account for the fact that while so fragmentary, at once imperfect and redundant, its several parts fall naturally into their places in the social framework of that early period.   We saw also in § 21 that the priest was a village officer exercising judicial functions.   He, therefore, is the depository of the

Different Thorahs.

"Thorah," the traditional "custom" of his village. But the customs of villages differ ; and there is every reason to suppose that they differed in the villages of Israel.   In fact, if the various parts of the country progressed at different rates (§ 29), differences of custom must inevitably have arisen.   The " Thorah,"

[1] Stenzler, *Âsvaldyana's Hausregeln*, pt. ii. p. 15.

therefore, must, while fundamentally alike, have differed in detail in different parts of Israel. This is the result arrived at by Dr. Steinthal in a late number of the *Zeitschrift für Völkerpsychologie.* He remarked the curious repetitions in Deuteronomy of the same laws at irregular intervals, such, for instance, as verses 14, 15, 16, compared with verses 21, 22, 23 of chap. xii., and showed that by careful arrangement much of Deuteronomy might be made to fall into some half-dozen smaller codes.[1] To examine the accuracy of Dr. Steinthal's details would carry us beyond our present limits; but assuming them to be *Preserved in existing books.* fairly true, is it not very probable that we have then before us the sets of village or tribal customs out of which Deuteronomy was compiled?

This brings us at once to the question of the legis- *Legislative phenomena in Hindu law books.* lative aspect of the books. Here, I think, more assistance might be gained than has been gained hitherto from the Hindu law-books which have been quoted in the course of this essay, viz., Manu, Yâjnavâlkya, Nârada, and the two in vol. ii. of the *Sacred Books of the East.* Relatively to each other, Manu, Yâjna-vâlkya, and Nârada are in chronological sequence. No one, I think, can read Manu without seeing that the book has grown by successive accretions of judicial matter. Its editors have annotated it, demurred to various points in it, endeavoured to twist others to their own views; but in the main it still remains a traditional collection. Yâjnavâlkya, which is next in chronological order, differs from Manu in extent,

---

[1] *Z. für V.-Psychologie,* xi. 1-28.

being far more condensed and systematised. In matter, too, Yâjnavâlkya differs from Manu, but preserves the sequence, and, for the most part, the substance of Manu, to such an extent as to show that Manu was the standard from which the later book was drawn up. Nârada exhibits similar features. Systematisation has changed the appearance of the book entirely from that of Manu, and yet much remains of the spirit of Manu, and even an appreciable portion of Manu's language. And for all that it is so systematised, Dr. Jolly, the translator, lays stress upon the fact that its enactments "are not mere theoretical rules and precepts, but such as have doubtless been actually administered.[1]

Limitation of legislation by primitive traditions.

My point in quoting this illustration is to show the extent to which the "customary law" limited the efforts of the later legislators. So far as regards annotation and addition of newer matter, they were at liberty; but they were not at liberty with regard to the traditional matter. In viewing, therefore, the Pentateuchal records, we require to bear in mind their double aspect—as regards their matter, primitive and of traditional authority; as regards their form, not necessarily so. But it should always be remembered that the matter was that which later innovators could alter very little, if at all, except in so far as the people had already advanced beyond the earlier custom.

Thus it grows clear that the form must always be controlled to a great extent by the matter, and that

---

[1] *Nârada's Institutes*, pref. xxvii.

a study of the matter must precede the study of the
form ; for not until one knows the meaning and
scope of a law can one judge fairly of the extent to
which it may have been glossed or revised by later
hands. Such a preliminary study this essay purports
to be. Taking the Pentateuchal laws as they stand,
we have examined them as one might examine the
laws of any other ancient code ; we have compared
them with the laws of other peoples ; we have arranged them in chronological sequence as they arose ;
and thus we have endeavoured to exhibit the forces
which made Hebrew society what it was. If this
aim has been at all accomplished, if some light has
been thrown upon the pre-prophetic period of Hebrew
history—that period of which no certain literary
record now remains ; if to some extent we have
reconstructed early Hebrew life, then

δ ὠφείλομεν ποιῆσαι πεποιήκαμεν.

INDEX.

G

INDEX.

---

www.ingramcontent.com/pod-product-compliance
Lightning Source LLC
Chambersburg PA
CBHW030621270326
41927CB00007B/1274